A MALTESE ANTHOLOGY

KV-267-887

A MALTESE ANTHOLOGY

COMPILED BY

A. J. ARBERRY

OXFORD
AT THE CLARENDON PRESS
1960

Oxford University Press, Amen House, London E.C.4

GLASGOW NEW YORK TORONTO MELBOURNE WELLINGTON
BOMBAY CALCUTTA MADRAS KARACHI KUALA LUMPUR
CAPE TOWN IBADAN NAIROBI ACCRA

© *Oxford University Press 1960*

C 6202764 6

HERTFORDSHIRE
COUNTY LIBRARY
1795172
892 789

PRINTED IN GREAT BRITAIN
AT THE UNIVERSITY PRESS, OXFORD
BY VIVIAN RIDLER
PRINTER TO THE UNIVERSITY

PREFACE

Two winter months spent in Malta not only restored me after a stubborn illness, but also enriched me with a new experience of which this volume is the first-fruits. For both I am deeply grateful to Malta and the Maltese people.

My thanks are due first to the man whose constant help and encouragement alone enabled me to attempt this task, my good friend and colleague Professor J. Aquilina, Professor of Maltese in the Royal University of Malta. He gave most generously of his little spare time to assist me to choose my extracts from Maltese literature, and to understand what I had chosen. Through him I had the privilege of meeting the leading authors of Malta, whose ready willingness to allow me to present them in English is a further charge on my gratitude.

My Faculty enabled me to engage the services of a learned young Maltese scholar, Father Prosper Grech, whose share in this enterprise was at least as great as my own. For his unfailing and most valuable assistance, and for his cheerful and inspiring companionship, I am exceeding grateful.

Finally, I offer my thanks to the Delegates of the Oxford University Press for undertaking to publish this book, and to their staff for their help in seeing it through the press.

It is my earnest hope that this modest work will make a contribution towards better Anglo-Maltese understanding, by bringing before the English-reading public the voice and heart of Malta, the expression of Malta's long and glorious history and of its people's ideals and aspirations.

A. J. A.

CONTENTS

CONTENTS

PART THREE
Poetry

CONTENTS

INTRODUCTION

MALTESE literature is a comparatively modern development, having a history of little more than a century, and an effective history of considerably less than
that time: the Maltese language itself is certainly
ancient, though too little has survived from earlier
ages to make possible a systematic analysis of its
origins and evolution. The most authoritative account
of the present state of knowledge on this subject is
contained in a paper entitled *Maltese as a Mixed
Language*, written by Professor J. Aquilina who
occupies with great distinction the Chair of Maltese in
the Royal University of Malta. This paper was published as recently as January 1958 in the third volume
of the *Journal of Semitic Studies*, and the following
abstract is here presented with the author's permission.

The language we speak in Malta, like the language
the English speak in England, is made up of various
word-elements which originated from various sources.
A mixed language presupposes a mixed history—the
history of a people which has had a variety of social and
historical environments each of which has moulded
the texture of the language spoken. A mixed language
is a fused language and if one may speak of a fused
language one can speak of a fused society. Maltese, like
English mixed from various sources, basically Semitic,
superstructurally Romance, is an organic linguistic
whole.

The historical reconstruction of the language is by
its very nature sociological. We go as far back as we

can in time where we meet the earliest language-makers. There are ten historical periods, ten foreign rulers who politically and linguistically affected the destiny of the Maltese Archipelago. Linguistic civilization in Malta has a very ancient tradition. Sometimes the linguistic evidences are not available and the degree of civilization is surmised from the historical remains of vanished peoples. The finest historical remains of Malta and Gozo are prehistoric. These are the world-famous megalithic temples, unique in the world. The evidence is purely in stone and not in language. However, the degree of civilization which prevailed in prehistoric Malta about 2000 B.C. presupposes a high degree of linguistic self-expression: but that is all that we can say.

The next historical period is that of the Phoenicians and the Carthaginians (1500 B.C.–216 B.C.). This period seems to have exercised an unbalanced effect on the critical judgment of a good number of Maltese historians and linguists. There is no evidence of any Phoenician or Punic remains in our language, and it is idle to attribute to the Phoenicians or Carthaginians the authorship of the Semitic vocabulary of the language. This does not mean that Punic was not spoken in Malta before and during the Roman domination, which followed that of the Carthaginians. As a matter of fact we have outside evidence that at the time of St. Paul's shipwreck Malta was inhabited by a Punic community. I must also add that when I say that the Semitic basis of Maltese has nothing in it exclusively I do not deny *a priori* the possibility of Punic lexical substrata. As a matter of fact, Maltese has hundreds of Semitic words which, as far as we can say now, are local formations but some of which may as well be semantic residues of a previous Semitic vocabulary. However, for our purpose we must exclude also the Phoenicians and the

Carthaginians from the list of historical participants in the formation of Maltese as it is spoken today.

The Phoenician era, historical evidences of which consist of a few inscriptions found in various parts of Malta, was followed by that of the Romans under whom Malta, either before or after 218 B.C., had its own senate and assembly on the Athenian model, with the right of sending legates to Rome. But again linguistically, the Roman era does not count at all as far as the Maltese language is concerned. The few semiticized Latin words we have came to Malta with Arabic from *Ifriqiya*, a centre of Greco-Latin culture before the violent onrush of Arabic conquest.

So far we have mentioned three peoples, historical realities but linguistic nonentities as far as the construction of Maltese is concerned. But now come the Arabs, who conquered the Maltese archipelago in A.D. 870 and lost it to the Normans 220 years later. The Arabs are linguistically the most important people that ever managed the affairs of the country. But how much do we know politically about the Arabs in Malta? Strangely enough, we know next to nothing. We have no information about their social life in our island, their attitude to the native population, to the long-established Christian church. The answers to these and other questions have to be drawn from the evidence of the more detailed history of the Arabs in Sicily of which Malta was a province. The strongest evidence of Arabic influence we have is the language we speak; for there is no doubt that, allowing for a number of peculiarities and erratic developments, Maltese is structurally an Arabic dialect.

When the Arabs conquered Malta they found a native community, and a Christian church that must have had its own non-Arabic language. What happened to the language spoken by the native Maltese? The answer is: precisely what happened to the indigenous language of North Africa and Egypt. How do we explain that the Arabs did not likewise replace Sicilian by Arabic? The answer is: that is really a question of numbers. There were more Sicilians than Arabs— many more; and Sicily being a much larger island was in a better position to safeguard her linguistic independence. In Malta, a comparatively much smaller island, the Arabs just succeeded in forcing their language on the small native community who, however, being a Christian community, must have retained linguistic semantic functions associated with their own religion and manner of life.

What kind of vocabulary did the Arabs leave behind them so deep-rooted that after more than 900 years of complete severance from Arabic linguistic sources it remains the basic structure of Maltese as spoken today, in spite of the large-scale admixture from Sicily and Italy? A complete modern dictionary is bound to include several hundreds of non-Arabic words. But the dictionary of A. E. Caruana lists words of Semitic origin only. According to Dr. Micallef's estimate the total number of words of every sort registered by Caruana amounts to 9,947. This piece of word-frequency does not indicate a very extensive Semitic vocabulary. The Semitic word-lore is largely outnumbered by the loanwords, very much as loanwords outnumber the Anglo-Saxon words of the English dictionary. On the other hand, the Semitic vocabulary of Maltese is extensive enough to express the manifold ideas and contexts of ordinary human life, the world of primitive, elemental ideas, man's natural world of feeling and reacting. This explains why Maltese poets find it so easy to employ words of Semitic origin.

The Semitic vocabulary of Maltese indicates ethnic admixture within the Aghlabid tribe that conquered Malta, who from their capital at Qayrawan dominated in their century of power (800–909) the mid-Mediterranean. The linguistic conquest of the Arabic tongue over the native languages of the subjugated peoples in North Africa inevitably created peculiar linguistic features of berberized Arabic and arabicized Berber. The new Arabic-speaking Moslems from *Ifriqiyah* made their dialectal contribution to the Maltese vocabulary. There are also in Maltese a few Arabic words the meanings of which seem to indicate direct or indirect Syrian admixtures. The Arabs brought with them from *Ifriqiyah* a few Latin words in arabicized form. There is in Maltese a sprinkling of words whose meanings seem to agree with those of corresponding words in Hebrew more than with those of Arabic. Even inside Arabic Maltese one can detect two or three linguistic strains which contributed to the admixture of early Maltese as a Semitic language.

There is no doubt that the Arabs laid the foundations of the language. They gave our ancestors a working functional vocabulary which helped them to make themselves mutually intelligible. That after their departure from Malta the vocabulary they left us had to be supplemented from outside sources was only natural, but the remarkable fact is that while loanwords from Sicily and Italy were mainly nouns, adjectives and verbs, the grammatical structure of the language, though it suffered considerable changes like other Arabic dialects, did on the whole maintain intact the principal features of the Semitic group. The main framework on which hang the hundreds of word-patterns, remained Arabic.

The Normans conquered Malta in 1090. With the

Norman conquest began a new era of linguistic accretions. These people spoke a language which was completely different from Arabic. They came to Malta from Sicily and brought Sicilian with them, and as the new masters of the Maltese Archipelago they began to exercise considerable phonetic and lexical influences on the language of the natives. But while the Arabs had practically imposed their language on the people, the Normans merely affected the vocabulary of the people and its phraseology. By the time they had conquered Malta, the Maltese language had already integrated itself with the mental speech-habits of the people and it seems that in spite of the common bond of Christianity the Normans and the Maltese kept linguistically apart. Then we assume feudal lords from Sicily settled in Malta and, mixing with the people, introduced gradually a number of their own native words into the language. But though the feudal lords were the masters, the language of the people continued to exercise linguistic supremacy, retaining its native structure and phonology, while at the same time it went on borrowing as many new words as were needed to express new ideas, new actions and new objects. In this historically very interesting period began the large-scale admixture of Maltese, which ceased to be completely Arabic till it gradually became a unique language mixed from Norman sources and in time from the linguistic stocks of the foreign rulers that followed the Normans. The Romance vocabulary must have been progressively added to by the Angevins during the period of Charles of Anjou (1266–83), the Aragonese (1283–1410), and the Castilians (1412–1530), when Malta was ceded to the Order of St. John. Arabic linguistic influence lasted till 1224 when Frederick expelled the Arabs from Malta.

The Order of St. John, which lasted from 1530 to

1798, must have more than trebled the frequency of Romance loanwords. The members of this semi-military Order were recruited from the aristocracy of Europe, and with them and their relatives thousands of new words must have flowed into the island. It is a strong indication of foreign social influence in Malta that the bishops of the church were at that time, and continued to be till the end of the Order, mainly Sicilian ecclesiastics. Likewise Sicilian were the notaries public, a strong foreign influence but not strong enough to overcome the resistance of the native language and customs.

In 1798 Napoleon took Malta by storm, and as there were already many Jacobins and pro-French partisans in the Order, the resistance put up by the last Grand Master of the Order was practically futile. The rule of the French was brief and hectic, linguistically of little or no account. The few Maltese words of French origin that we have in the language may go back to this period. There was a two years' siege in which the Maltese held the French at bay and with British help forced the French garrison to surrender (September 1800). A short time after, the Maltese Congress invited His Britannic Majesty to accept the sovereignty of the Maltese islands.

For many years the English language did not enjoy the important place it enjoys now. Its importance was overshadowed by the Italian language, which was inherited from the former Latin masters and continued to be used for many years by the State and Church till the people, whose education had been long neglected, began to question the supremacy of Italian as an official language in Malta and, after many political vicissitudes, Maltese took the place of Italian as an official language of the administration and the law courts. Italian is still the official language of the

Archbishop's Curia but sooner or later it is bound to be replaced by the people's language. Maltese is already being used in several official notices published by the Curia. The lexical element of English origin is very limited as compared with that of Italian and Sicilian origin. The reasons are partly social and partly linguistic. By social reasons I understand the aloofness of the English community in Malta from the native inhabitants; by linguistic reasons I understand the inherent phonological and morphological differences between the two languages. However, English linguistic influences are now increasing and likewise the impact of the English language on Maltese is now being felt much more than it used to be in the past.

There have always been language-makers in Malta. The process of ethnic and linguistic admixture is continuous. The Maltese language, like the English language, having succeeded in blending heterogeneous linguistic elements within the framework of its native mechanics, has acquired a greater power of self-expression to supply the demand of an intellectually active society continually at grips with new ideas and new orientations, a mixed language combining its own linguistic virtues with those of the people from whom we have borrowed new sounds and new word-patterns.

The isolation of the dialect spoken in Malta from all other forms of spoken Arabic, and above all from the classical language of the Koran and the sacred and profane literature of the Arabs, led to consequences even more interesting than the evolution of a mixed speech. Classical Arabic must have been the prestige language in Malta during the somewhat brief Arab domination; for although no books or other paper documents from that period have survived, we can rely upon the evidence of a certain number of inscriptions, notably the fine Majmuna tombstone described by A. Cremona as 'a marble slab beautifully cut with Kufic raised characters, bearing the date 569 of the Hegira (1173 A.D.) when the Arab domination in the Islands had already ceased'. This famous stone was discovered in a field in the smaller island of Gozo, and has not been matched so far by anything unearthed in Malta itself; but it is reasonable to suppose that further excavation, especially of the Arab cemetery outside the gates of Mdina, will bring to light more proof that literary Arabic was well understood down to the end of the twelfth century. A census made in 1119 found 836 Saracen families living in the archipelago, as against 250 Christian and 33 Jewish. The Christians of that period also used Arabic, to judge by the number of Arabic words employed in modern Maltese for expressing purely Christian concepts. I have seen an ancient ikon, of no artistic merit but bearing an inscription in Arabic, which was discovered in a barn on a remote farm in the interior of Malta.

That any Ibn Quzman or al-Shushtari should have flourished in Arab Malta, so bold as to swim against the strong current of classical Arabic and to compose dialect poetry, is on the face of things extremely improbable. Maltese did not emerge upon the stage of literature until the seventeenth century, or so existing records suggest. But whereas throughout all the Arab and Muslim world, even down to the present day, the language of literature has remained classical Arabic, uniquely in Malta an Arabic dialect has freely developed into a literary language. Maltese thus alone affords a pattern of what might have happened from Morocco to Iraq, had the local dialects overcome and usurped the authority of the classical idiom. Maltese is the only 'Romance' language to evolve in the Arabic-speaking world.

In this anthology of Maltese literature the attempt has been made to illustrate the main stages through which Maltese has passed in the course of its short history as a written language. The first of its three sections is made up of folk-material presented in Maltese and English. It has been assumed that pro-verbs, folk-tales, and popular rhymes are apt to exhibit the language in its most primitive and un-sophisticated form. Of course even these are bound to have been affected by changes wrought in vernacular speech during the passage of time; but in the absence of any authentic record of pre-literary Maltese, these selections drawn from the work of Maltese scholars may be accepted as approximate specimens of medieval Maltese. It will be observed that the vocabulary is almost wholly Semitic. The tale of the Seven Citron-Maidens has been translated previously by Miss Margaret A. Murray and Mrs. L. Galea, widow of the Maltese author A. M. Galea. For the text of 'The Fisherman's Son', hitherto unpublished, I am in-debted to Mr. G. Cassar-Pullicino who collected it. The researches of this able and enthusiastic folklorist have also been utilized in the small selection of riddles. It is unnecessary to remark that similar examples of folk-material are to be found in many other Arabic dialects.

The second and third sections of the anthology trace

the development of literary Maltese during the last
century or so. There is one exception: the section on
poetry opens with a unique relic from the seventeenth
century discussed in more detail later. The pieces
have been chosen not only to illustrate the work of the
most esteemed authors, but also for their value in
depicting the Maltese scene in its various aspects. The
history of the islands and of their people is recap-
tured in factual or fictional descriptions of outstanding
political events and social circumstances. The per-
vasive religious atmosphere represents faithfully a
people passionately attached to Catholic Christianity
and naturally devout: the Maltese are the only Arabic-
speaking Christians to have produced a worthy and
vigorous Christian literature. Some of the devotional
poems are quite remarkable: the work of Dun Karm
in particular is outstanding in any context.

Because these writings were intended for the
Maltese public, they are innocent of any propaganda
slant aimed at presenting 'Malta's case' to the outside
world. They may therefore be studied as authentic
expressions of Maltese life, Maltese pride, Maltese
humour, Maltese pathos, Maltese values, Maltese
aspirations, the Maltese point of view. The ardent
nationalism of very small communities—Malta's
population is only 350,000, that of any average in-
dustrial city in Europe—seems fantastic and unreal to
those fortunate or unfortunate to be born in large
countries: this anthology will make Maltese nationalism more comprehensible, the tragedy of Malta's
inviability more poignant.

As one turns the pages of Malta's history, one is

seized with a sense of greatness out of all proportion to the numerically insignificant forces engaged. Cradle of Mediterranean culture—so the discoveries of the archaeologists tend to suggest—Malta has played a part, sometimes a very vital part, in the drama of rising and falling empires from the dawn of recorded time. If her share in the fortunes of imperial Rome was slight, nevertheless here St. Paul was shipwrecked, according to credible report, in A.D. 60, and Malta is understandably proud of a continuous tradition of Christian witness going back to the very beginnings of the faith. The church founded by St. Paul survived the Arab conquest: whereas Islam destroyed Christianity in the neighbouring province where the great Augustine lived and taught, and reduced the followers of Jesus to the status of a tolerated minority in Egypt and all the Levant, in *Malta Fidelissima* the Cross triumphed over the Crescent.

The coming of the Knights of St. John from Rhodes to Malta invested the island with an international significance undiminished down to the present time. Bulwark of Europe at bay against the Saracens, Malta stood siege against greatly superior Turkish armaments and won a decisive and bloody victory in 1565. Thereafter the Order, attracting to the island the flower of Europe's nobility, lived a metropolitan life in Malta. Fine hospices and splendid residences were built; noble churches adorned the skyline; some of Europe's most famous architects and artists were employed to beautify the Most Catholic Island.

The defeat of the Turkish invaders was the first

great moment of Maltese national pride. The second moment was the expulsion of Napoleon's garrison. Many had welcomed the suppression of the Order by the French forces, still marching in the name of liberty; but Napoleon alienated all sympathy in the island by his desecration of the ancient cathedral and the excesses of his licentious soldiery, and the appearance in Maltese waters of Nelson's fleet was hailed as a deliverance. Malta rose as one man against the French, and of her own strong desire sought the protection of the British Crown. Nearly a century and a half later, Malta's third great moment arrived—her heroic stand against the combined air armadas of Nazi Germany and Fascist Italy which won for her the admiration of the world and the unique award of the George Cross. These three triumphs against powerful enemies recur again and again as patriotic themes in Maltese literature: they are moments of which Malta is justly proud.

Language has been a strong factor in the growth of national consciousness in Malta. The old aristocracy came to the island chiefly from Sicily, and therefore felt Italian to be their mother-tongue. This tradition persisted to as recently as 1940, and was naturally encouraged by Mussolini, who found the British occupation of Malta, commanding the narrows of *Mare Nostrum*, to be intolerable. Fascist propaganda even made the crude attempt to suggest that Maltese was in reality a dialect of Italian, but that line of approach did not get very far. It was therefore the old aristocracy, and by no means the British administrators (who indeed viewed the scene with the most aloof indifference), that impeded the emergence of Maltese as the national language of Malta. The experience of Vassalli, the father of the Maltese language, is described movingly in the essay by A. Cremona, who has himself contributed much to the development of Maltese both as a grammarian and as a poet and dramatist. It is thus not surprising that the language should be a favourite theme of many writers; as a symbol of the struggle for national emancipation it has been accorded almost sacrosanct status.

The sea naturally dominates the mind and imagination of every Maltese, even as it controls the very life of the islands. Its changing moods, its gently lapping or furiously lashing Malta's rocky shores, have inspired many fine poems. Equally the golden sunshine of the long summer, and the open expanse of the skies crowded by night with a countless multitude of brilliant stars, constitute well-loved topics. The countryside, for all its inevitable limitations, is felt to offer a blessed refuge from the crowded towns with their narrow streets: the Maltese craving for the infinite distances is an escape from the sense of claustrophobia familiar to all who have lived in the islands for any length of time.

Though Malta lies so close to the coasts of North Africa that its air is charged with the torrid dust of the Sahara whenever the hated sirocco blows, no Maltese thinks of himself as other than a European. The Arab connexion, perpetuated in the language and only too apparent to those Maltese who have migrated to Tunisia or Egypt, is steadfastly renounced. Malta is an ancient and integral part of the Christian West: for religious guidance it looks to Rome, for political institutions to London. While the older generation of writers depended in the main on Italian models, the younger generation have now been brought up on Shakespeare and Bacon, Wordsworth and Shelley, Tennyson and Dickens, T. S. Eliot and Ezra Pound. Whatever political surprises the future may hold in store, it seems certain that Malta's strong link with Christian civilization will prove indissoluble.

Jean Quintin's *Descriptio Insulae Melitae* (Leiden, 1536) furnishes our earliest evidence for the existence of a Maltese language. Lists of Maltese words and phrases are contained in Hieronymus Megiser's *Propugnaculum Europae* (1611), Philip Skipton's *Account of a Journey* (made in 1663–4), and the *Hierolexicon* of Domenico and Carlo Magri (1675). The oldest surviving specimen of actual writing in Maltese appears to be the ode composed by the naturalist Gio Francesco Bonamico in honour of Grand Master Cottoner (MS. 144 in the Royal Malta Library). The text of this poem, reduced to modern orthography, is printed in the preface to G. Aquilina's *Il-Muża Maltija*; the translation here offered is reasonably close and aims to bring out the simple language but sophisticated style of the original. When we read the poem we are immediately reminded of the long tradition of panegyric in Arabic literature; the conceit that Cottoner's presence converts winter cold to summer warmth is not unworthy of a Mutanabbi. But presumably the immediate model was Italian.

A number of grammars and dictionaries of Maltese are known to have been compiled between 1600 and

1730. The oldest surviving prose-work in Maltese is a collection of sermons composed from 1739 onwards by the Rev. Ignazio Saverio Mifsud (MS. Misc. 48); A. Cremona states that 'their language is impregnated with italianisms'. In 1750 Canon Gio-Pietro Francesco Sultana (Agius De Soldanis) published his *Della Lingua Punica presentamente usata dai Maltesi*, thus giving currency to the erroneous view that Maltese is a survival of Punic; he also sought to trace a link between Maltese and Etruscan. To him we owe an imaginary dialogue which is an invaluable specimen of eighteenth-century colloquial Maltese. In 1790 Vassalli published the first of his many works on Maltese, the *Alfabeto Maltese*, followed in 1791 by his *Mylsen Phoenico-Punicum* and in 1796 by his *Ktyb-yl-Klym Malti*. Meanwhile Bellermann and Gesenius turned their attention to the study of Maltese, emulated in 1829 by the great Silvestre De Sacy who, while praising Vassalli's work, enunciated the theory that Maltese was not Phoenician but an offshoot of Arabic. In the face of bitter opposition Vassalli persevered with his labours to adapt the spoken language to a literary form, and produced among other books a Maltese translation of the Gospels and Acts (1829) on a commission from the Church Missionary Society. R. Watts of London had already in 1822 published a version of St. John made by G. M. Canolo, a knife-grinder. A Maltese reading-book by F. Vella and G. M. Pulis appeared at Leghorn in 1824.

The first half of the nineteenth century saw the slow beginnings of the literary movement which reached its culmination during the second quarter of the twentieth. A sonnet dating from 1838 already exhibits a certain technical maturity, though the thought and style of expression are still curiously reminiscent of Arabia. Canon L. Mifsud Tommasi (?1795–1879) in his earlier years composed poetry in Italian and hymns in Maltese. Richard Taylor, who was born at Bormla in 1818, lived for a number of years in Egypt and returned to Malta to open a tobacconist's shop; this venture failing, he became a journalist. He composed a number of religious books, and made a metrical version of the Psalms; he also translated part of Dante's *Divina Commedia*. Gan-Anton Vassallo (1817–68), sometime Professor of Italian in the Royal University, wrote several works of history and biography and two volumes of verse; he also published in 1852 an ambitious epic of the war against the Turks, *Il-Ġifen Tork*. Author of the celebrated patriotic poem beginning 'Int sabiħa, o Malta tagħna', he may be considered as the first Maltese writer of outstanding talent. Other important figures of the nineteenth and early twentieth centuries include Gio-Batta Falzon, best remembered for his Maltese–Italian–English dictionary; Dwardu Cachia, a fertile poet who in addition translated a portion of Camoens's *Os Lusiados*; and the greatly revered Ġuże' Muscat-Azzopardi (1853–1927), poet, novelist, and critic, by profession a lawyer, first President of the Għaqda tal-Kittieba tal-Malti (Society of Maltese Authors).

The most acute problem, along with the formulation of Maltese grammar and syntax and the registration of Maltese lexicography, was the establishment of a satisfactory alphabet and a uniform system of spelling. Vassalli had devoted much time and considerable acuteness to this question, but his pioneering efforts not unnaturally did not satisfy his successors. Maltese has certain sounds not found in any European language, and it was the representation of these that provoked most controversy. A valuable summary of the various proposals made during the nineteenth century, proposals some of which included the introduction of a few Arabic letters to indicate the exotic sounds, is given by A. Cremona in his *Historical Review of the Maltese Language* (1945). The debate continued well into the present century, and at times orthography even became a bitter political issue. In 1920 a committee was appointed to work out an agreed system, and their final recommendations, reached after a fair degree of compromise, were at last in 1934 recognized as the official standard spelling. A. Cremona's comments on the present Maltese alphabet are well worthy of study, coming as they do from an eminent grammarian who has contributed greatly to the shaping of the language in our times.

The solution of the problem for standardizing the Maltese orthography lay mainly in adapting a script which tallied with the existing prejudices and which, at the same time, might be reasonably consistent with the morphological nature of the language as now spoken. In framing its alphabet the 'Għaqda tal-Kittieba tal-Malti' seems to have acted with this particular point in view. So far it has been realized that under the present favourable conditions in the local system of education and constitutional status of the Island, the Għaqda's alphabet and its morphological system of transliteration is the most fortunate among nearly thirty-two alphabets which had been proposed and used since the seventeenth century up to 1924.

Undoubtedly, the Għaqda's system may be considered as an ideal one for practical and popular purposes and, to a certain extent, the most adaptable for scholastic purposes also; but it is quite obvious that for purposes of etymological studies it may not be adequate and in treatises of a purely philological nature a transliteration based on more scientific principles as now generally recognized by orientalists should preferably be used. As however all emphatic dentals and sibilants have entirely disappeared from the spoken language, such a newly devised alphabet will have to be limited to the same number of symbols as in the plan of Vassalli's alphabet. Such a purely scientific alphabet may only be, therefore, confined to the transliteration of such specimens of Maltese words as are compared with other semitic analogues, as different from the official current transcription used in popular, literary and Government publications on the basis of the Għaqda's alphabet so far used. On the other hand, it must be owned, an alphabet devised on a purely scientific basis is hardly adaptable for ordinary use owing to its pedantic nature and, consequently, it cannot be expected to replace the common one. But what is hardly conceivable of adoption in ordinary life becomes, inversely, quite possible in the limited sphere of scientific life.

The Maltese language has now proved itself to be an instrument capable of expressing the widest range of feelings and ideas with freedom, unreserve, and at times great eloquence. It is a far cry from the rude patois scorned by Faris al-Shidyaq, that brilliant but arrogant Syrian polymath, when he visited the islands in the 1830's, to the mature and sensitive language of Dun Karm and Cremona, Aquilina and Vassallo. Maltese has achieved within a century what English required several hundreds of years to accomplish, thanks to the courage, enthusiasm, and concentrated purpose of a comparatively small number of dedicated men. Out of a poor dialect, banished from cultured homes to the kitchen and the fields, it has been transformed into a literary language enjoying all the prestige inherent in high style. This it has done without losing touch with the idiom of the masses. Education, rapidly extended in recent decades, is overcoming illiteracy and rearing a generation to whom literary Maltese is the natural medium of self-expression. The popular press and local broadcasting contribute much to the spread of language consciousness among the less literate classes. On the other hand poets and writers, dissatisfied by easy recourse to words borrowed from Italian to express new conceptions or to describe new objects, have gone to the villages and recovered from the mouths of the peasants many ancient roots well suited to convey the required meanings. With the common sense characteristic of the Maltese this enriching of the national vocabulary from within has not been accomplished in any doctrinaire or xenophobic spirit; the Maltese speech, like the Maltese people, is instinctively hospitable and continues to welcome from abroad all words which have a real contribution to make to the language.

Those interested in the phenomenon of linguistic borrowings, so potent a factor in making English what it is, will find instructive Professor Aquilina's pamphlet *A Comparative Study of Mixed Maltese* (1949) from which the following paragraphs have been abstracted.

Loan words in Maltese are so numerous that they feature in most departments of our social life, especially those that are the products of a later post-Arabic civilization. Romance loan words, generally Mediaeval Sicilian or Italian, are used for the names of:—

1. *most sacred things*, including religion, its rites, celebrations, Church and ecclesiastical vestments. In this connection, very interesting are the religious names of Syriac origin.

2. *the twelve months of the year*, wind directions except *nofs inhar*, south; *riħ isfel*, south-east wind, and *riħ fuq*, north-west wind.

3. *a considerable number of parental relationships*. It is interesting to note in this connection that while the Maltese name for 'father', *missier*, is of Romance origin, the name for 'mother', *omm*, is Semitic. Very likely, as in England, the Normans that conquered Malta married native wives, each retaining the native word for 'father' and 'mother' respectively.

4. *most medicaments* as porga, ingwent, etc.

5. *most objects usually associated with the* 'City' though the city itself and its bastions have Semitic names.

6. *most objects connected with the household including the dining room and the bed room*, though the house itself and several of its constituent structures as the 'roof', **'the** floor', etc. have Semitic names.

7. *most objects connected with liquors, victuals and kitchen* excepting the primitive kinds of food such as *bajd*, eggs, *ħobż*, bread, etc.

8. *a good number of fruits and fruit trees*, though as a whole these are predominantly Semitic.

9. *the greater number of wild trees, flowers, and odiferous plants; wild quadrupeds; birds and some of the domestic fowls.*

10. *plants and seeds* but the majority are Semitic.

11. *fish and shell fish*, a majority of which is Semitic.

12. *most metals, minerals* and *precious stones*.

13. most objects connected with *the navy and navigation* or shipping in general, *parts of ships*, the *army, military* and *naval ranks*.

Interesting exceptions are: ʻifen (North African), ship; qlugħ, sails; moqdief, oar; and mirkeb (obsolete if ever used), ship. The origin of dgħajsa is unknown, but it is very likely Romance. It occurs also in Spanish Arabic. As for 'armiral', the word, though ultimately Arabic, was directly borrowed from the Italian. Dejma is Semitic Maltese for 'standing army'.

14. most objects connected with *entertainments* as *ballu*, ball, compared with which Semitic Maltese 'żfin', dancing, is general, including *sports*, names of which are generally English as football, goal, foul, tennis, etc.

15. most objects connected with *education* in general excepting such primitive names as *ktieb*, book; *qara*, to read; *kiteb*, to write; *għadd*, to count; *għallem*, to teach; *tgħallem*, to learn; *tagħlim*, teaching or learning, etc.

16. most *occupations* such as needlework, objects connected with it, *trades, professions, the arts* and their respective *technical words*.

17. most men's and women's *clothes, toilet,* and *drapery*.

18. (a) *multiplicative adjectives* as *singlu, doppju*, (translatable periphrastically as *għal darbtejn*); (b) *adjectives of dimensions* except a few as *għoli*, high; *wiesa'*, wide; *twil*, long, etc.; (c) *numerical fractions* except

nofs, half, *robu'*, one fourth, plural *rbiegħ*, and *egħxur*, tenths or tithes. *Composite fractions* are only partially Romance as *tliet* (Semitic Maltese), *ottavi* (Romance Maltese), three eighths.

19. *most implements* and *tools*; but there is also a good number of Semitic ones connected with a primitive civilization.

20. rules of Maltese *prosody* and *scansion*, generally Italian but not without some English influences.

To these we must add the various Romance influences that have modified the phonetics including intonation, phonology, morphology and syntax of Semitic Maltese respectively.

In this anthology specimens have been given of as wide a variety of styles as possible. The prose section includes straightforward historical narrative from the nineteenth and twentieth centuries; literary appreciation and criticism; Christian homiletic; fiction also serving the purpose of sociological commentary; short stories illustrating different aspects of local life and feeling; a section from a detective novel with the National Museum as its background; and a playlet for broadcasting written in simple colloquial. It can I think be claimed that all these examples of Maltese writing, some quite unsophisticated and some highly stylized, are capable of being turned readily into acceptable English without sacrificing too much of their natural colour—a proof that the thought behind the expression is in every case solid and under firm control.

The poetry traces a pattern of development with which we are familiar when studying the poetry of any European language; except that in Maltese the process of change has been telescoped into a very few decades. Beginning with simple folk-rhymes which already appear to depend upon Italian for their prosody and scansion—though of course these features may have been superimposed upon a more primitive base now untraceable—we see the fixing of a classical style, quickly followed by a romantic reaction, then mixed classical and romantic, then neo-classical and neo-romantic, and finally free verse reflecting various contemporary schools of European poetry. A solitary exception to the Italianate prosody is provided by certain of the compositions of Mary Meylaq, born in Gozo in 1905 and now a schoolmistress, which are characterized by the monorhyme peculiar to Arabic poetry. As explained above, the poems have been selected not for their intrinsic merit alone, but also and especially for their relevance to the Maltese scene; many excellent pieces have been passed over because their themes are common to all poetry and because in their treatment of those themes no typically Maltese imagery is apparent.

It remains to add a few remarks on the present state and possible future evolution of Maltese literature. Some Maltese observers begin to feel that, with the realization of the main objective aimed at by the pioneers—the establishment of Maltese as the national language—the original and long-sustained impetus which gave rise to the modern literature is showing signs of having spent itself. While more people are writing good Maltese than ever before, and while every possible encouragement is being given to aspiring authors, there seems to be a growing sense of staleness, if not of exhaustion. Some of the young Maltese, particularly those whose inclinations are towards science and technology, tend to regard (or, what amounts in the end to the same thing, affect to regard) the study and practice of Maltese writing as a waste of time and effort. On the other hand it is only just to report the more optimistic view held by others, that Maltese literature is only in its prime and that great developments still lie ahead.

It is not irrelevant ro refer to the economics of Maltese authorship. Since the potential public for a Maltese novel or volume of verse is inevitably extremely small in comparison with the markets open to authors using the major languages of the world, and since printing and publication costs, in Malta as elsewhere, continue to increase, writing in Maltese can never in the nature of things be considered as a career, except possibly in journalism and broadcasting; and even these fields are very restricted and discouragingly unrewarding. Many Maltese today write excellent English, just as the learned Maltese of the past wrote excellent Italian. Dun Karm, the national poet, made his name as an Italian poet before he composed anything in Maltese. Ġorġ Zammit has written admirable English as well as Maltese poems. The citations from A. Cremona and Ġ. Aquilina included in this introduction beat witness to their complete mastery of scholarly English.

The temptation for the Maltese author of the future to express himself in English rather than Maltese will be very great. Malta may indeed produce her Conrads and Hsiungs. But the present unease may well be due to causes not peculiarly Maltese. Writers all over the world, in common with artists and musicians, acutely conscious of the intolerable burden of what their predecessors have achieved, search feverishly for new themes and new techniques. Politically and spiritually too the earth is in chaos; great driftings of power, immense economic and social upheavals, the constant threat of annihilation, the incredible prospect of the exploration of space—these incessant bombardments of incalculable events have shattered all accepted standards, rendered meaningless all traditional and most experimental forms of self-expression. Can order be restored out of man's present anarchy?

Insularity of outlook is the besetting temptation of all island peoples; and Malta is a very small island. It may therefore bring consolation—if poor consolation at that—to Malta's writers that some part of their predicament is common to all mankind. But Malta also faces its own problems, affecting seriously the future of Maltese authorship. Population pressure is already forcing out of the motherland many of its ablest sons and daughters. Migrants of the first generation may tenaciously retain their hold on the mother-tongue; the next generation will become assimilated into the communities of their adoption, and the authors among them will assuredly not write in Maltese. If independence is achieved, the price to be paid may prove overwhelming. Cultural isolation, following the severance of the Commonwealth link, might mean the death of Maltese literature.

Unfortunately these are by no means remote possibilities. The conscientious scholar, whose most earnest desire is to abstain from every form of political activity, cannot therefore exclude from his purview the likely cultural consequences of certain political developments. Having come to admire the Maltese people and what they have so heroically achieved in the realm of language and literature, and being sincerely anxious that that achievement should prove the foundations of a splendid edifice yet to be built and not an abandoned site, I cannot forbear to express the hope that Malta may remain for many years to come in close and fruitful association with Great Britain, and that she may continue to play her historic role as a bastion of Western civilization. Malta is more than a nation; nationhood of the narrow dimensions advocated by certain idealists would prove to be a straitjacket rather than a liberation. Malta, the Malta of the spirit, the Malta of the saints and seers, is international; her culture, to be meaningful, while remaining faithful to the splendid past and displaying itself in terms of the island home, will find its full expression as a voice in the choir of all mankind.

The infinite reaches of the universe are calling to Malta's writers of the future. They will not close their ears to that call.

PART ONE

Proverbs, Folk-tales
Popular Songs
Riddles

Proverbs

(1) Kliem ix-xiħ żomm fih.

(2) Min jittarraf jiġġarraf.

(3) La ddardarx l-għajn li trid tixrob minnha.

(4) Asaħħ kelmet il-Malti minn ħalfet is-Sultan.

(5) Min għandu sebgħu dritt minn xejn ma jibża'.

(6) Alla fina, aħna fih; kull ma jagħmel għalina, kull ma nagħmlu għalih.

(7) B'demm il-fqir ġid qatt ma jsir.

(8) Wieħed imut fis-sakra, u l-ieħor imut għal qatra.

(9) Min jorqod ma jaqbadx ħut.

(10) Ruħek lil Alla, ġismek lit-trab, ħwejġek lil niesek, għax hekk insab.

(11) Aktar ma tikber aktar titgħallem.

(12) Il-ħanżir jekk taqtagħlu denbu dejjem ħanżir jibqa'.

(13) Ma' min rajtek xebbahtak.

(14) Kul għal qalbek u imxi għal għajn in·nies.

(15) Min jobżoq lejn is-sema jiġi f'wiċċu.

(16) Għal musmar tilef in-nagħla.

Proverbs

(1) Hold fast to the words of the old man.

(2) Whoever walks on the edge (of a precipice) will (surely) fall down (it).

(3) Don't foul the spring from which you may want to drink.

(4) The word of a Maltese is more reliable than the oath of a king.

(5) A man with a straight finger has nothing to fear.

(6) God (is) within us, we (are) in Him; all He does is for us, all we do is for Him.

(7) By (shedding) the blood of the poor no good ever comes.

(8) One man dies of drunkenness, and another dies for (want of) a drop.

(9) A sleeping man catches no fish.

(10) Your soul (goes) to God, your body to the dust, your belongings to your people, for so things happen.

(11) The older you grow the more you learn.

(12) If you cut off the tail of a pig it will always remain a pig.

(13) I likened you to those I saw you with.

(14) Eat to your heart's content, and go (as) in the eyes of the public.

(15) Whoever spits towards the sky, it comes (down) in his (own) face.

(16) For the sake of a nail he lost the shoe.

(17) Aħjini l-lum u oqtolni għada.

(18) Min jagħmillek id-deni, agħmillu l-ġid.

(19) Hares tajjeb 'il darek u la tħallelx lil ġarek.

(20) Il-magħmul tqisu tista' iżda le ssewwih.

(21) Kelb rieqed la tqajmux.

(22) Għal ħabba jqaxxar qamla.

(23) Ara bint min hi biex tkun taf x'inhi.

(24) Min jistenna jithenna.

(25) Aħjar ħarba minn karba.

(26) Għal għira u għal għar il-fqir jitrekken ġod-dar.

(27) Min ma jistax jagħmel li jrid jagħmel li jista'.

(28) Għall-ħwietem u għall-imsielet il-lum baqgħet xejn ma kielet.

(29) L-ilma fil-bir ma jaqtax għatx.

(30) Ftehima bejn tnejn isseħħ f'jumejn; ftehima bejn tlieta teħtieġ xahrejn.

(31) Faħħar il-baħar u ibqa' fuq l-art.

(32) Min jitwieled tond ma jmutx kwadru.

(33) Għajnejn morda ma jridux dawl.

(34) Aħbar li ma taqbellekx toqgħodx tismagħha.

(35) Għarusa ġdida kull ma tmiss ifuħ.

(36) Agħder, għaliex ma tafx fiex tiġi.

(37) Min igħid li jrid, ikollu jisma' milli ma jridx.

(17) Revive me today and kill me tomorrow.

(18) Whoever does you ill, do him good.

(19) Guard well your house and don't make your neighbour a thief.

(20) What's done you can measure, but you can't put it right.

(21) Don't waken a sleeping dog.

(22) For the sake of a cent he will skin a louse.

(23) See whose daughter she is and you will know what she is.

(24) He who waits rejoices (in the end).

(25) Better to run away than to groan.

(26) For envy and for shame the poor man squats at home.

(27) Whoever can't do what he wants does what he can.

(28) For the sake of rings and ear-rings today she has eaten nothing.

(29) Water (still) in the well doesn't quench the thirst.

(30) An agreement between two people is reached in two days; an agreement between three requires two months.

(31) Praise the sea, and remain on dry land.

(32) He who is born round will not die square.

(33) Sore eyes can't stand the light.

(34) News that isn't welcome to you, don't stop and listen to.

(35) A new bride—whatever she touches smells sweet.

(36) Feel (for others), because you don't know where you will end up.

(37) Whoever says what he likes will have to hear what he doesn't like.

(38) Min ħalaqna jaf bina.
(39) Aħseb il-ħażin biex it-tajjeb ma jonqosx.
(40) Kull qalb trid oħra.
(41) Għajn ma tara(x) qalb ma tuġa'(x).
(42) Min jiekol il-laħma jeħtieġ iġerrem l-għadma.
(43) Kif tagħmel jagħmlulek.
(44) Il-bżonn iġagħlek tagħmel kollox.
(45) Il-flus jagħmlu l-flus, u d-dud jagħmel id-dud.
(46) Iż-żmien jagħti parir.
(47) M'hux kull min jagħti fuq sidru huwa qaddis.
(48) Agħtini xortija u itfagħni 'l-baħar.
(49) Fejn tħobb il-qalb jimxu r-riġlejn.
(50) Min jixtieq id-deni 'l ġaru jiġih f'daru.

(38) He who created us has knowledge of us.
(39) Expect the worst, so that the good may not be lacking.
(40) Every heart desires another.
(41) What the eye doesn't see the heart doesn't grieve over.
(42) He who eats the meat must (also) gnaw the bone.
(43) As you do to others, they will do to you.
(44) Necessity makes you do everything.
(45) Money breeds money, and worms breed worms.
(46) Time gives good advice.
(47) Not everyone who beats his breast is a saint.
(48) Give me my luck, and throw me in the sea.
(49) Where the heart yearns the feet will go.
(50) Whoever wishes evil to his neighbour, it will come into his own house.

Is-seba' Tronġiet Mewwija

DARBA kien hemm Sultan li ma kellux tfal. Dan għamel wegħda li jekk ikollu, jagħmel għajn taż-żejt għan-nies biex jeħduh b'xejn.

Is-sema bagħatlu sabi u s-Sultan żamm kelmtu: il-għajn taż-żejt għamilha quddiem il-palazz tiegħu. Din il-għajn damet tarmi sa kemm it-tifel kiber.

Darba meta kienet għoddha nixfet għal kollox, resqet fuqha mara xiħa u bdiet tlaqqat iż-żejt b'qoxra ta' bajda, mbagħad mill-qoxra tiġbru b'tajjara u t-tajjara tagħsarha ġewwa kus. Bin is-Sultan, li kien qiegħed jara dan kollu minn wara t-tieqa, beda jidħaq kemm jiflaħ, waddab żrara u farrak il-qoxra tal-bajda f'idejn ix-xiħa. Dina tħares ma' dwarha u ma tara lil ħadd; dak dejjem jidħaq; jitfa' żrara oħra, jolqot il-kus u jkissru. Din id-darba ix-xiħa lemħitu u qaltlu:

—Huwa inti? Jarrak tiżżewweġ is-seba' tronġiet mewwija! Meta dak semagħha mar għand missieru u qallu:

—Irrid niżżewweġ is-seba' tronġiet mewwija.

Is-Sultan ried ineħħilu dan il-ħsieb minn rasu; imma kien kollu għal xejn.

Telaq immela bin is-Sultan minn għand missieru u mar għal għonq it-triq. Iltaqa' ma' xiħ u qallu:

8

The Seven Citron-maidens

ONCE upon a time there was a king who had no children. He made a vow that if he had a child, he would make a fountain of oil for the people to take for nothing.

Heaven sent him a son, and the king kept his word. He made the oil-fountain right in front of his palace. The fountain went on flowing until the boy grew up.

One day, when the fountain had almost dried up for good, an old woman came up and started scooping up the oil into an egg-shell. Then she collected the oil from the shell with a wad of cotton and squeezed it into a little jug. The king's son, who was watching all this from behind the window, began to laugh like anything. He threw down a pebble and smashed the egg-shell in the woman's hands. The old woman looked all round, but couldn't see anyone. The boy kept on laughing; he threw another pebble, hit the jug and broke it to pieces. This time the old woman spied him and said:

'Oh, so it was you! The devil marry you to the seven citron-maidens!'

When the boy heard these words he went in to his father and said:

'I want to marry the seven citron-maidens.'

The king tried to put this idea out of his mind, but it was no use. The prince set out from his father's

9

—Is-sliem għalik, nann!

—Sewwa, wieġbu dak, sewwa għamilt tgħidli s-sliem għalik; għax kieku ma għidtlix, kont nibilgħek belgħa u nġerrgħek ġergħa.

—Nann, raġa' qallu t-tifel, fejn insib is-seba' tronġiet mewwija?

—Eh, x'ħaġa hija din, qallu; kemm ġew u ma reġgħux lura! Imma inti imxi 'l quddiem u ssib ieħor ixjeħ minni u egħref minni; jista' jkun li jgħidlek.

Dak qabad it-triq darb' oħra u sa fl-aħħar iltaqa' ma' xiħ ieħor. Malli lemħu qallu:

—Is-sliem għalik, nann!

—Sewwa għamilt, qallu x-xiħ, tgħidli is-sliem għalik; għax kieku ma għidtlix, kont nibilgħek belgħa u nġerrgħek ġergħa.

—Nann, qallu t-tifel, fejn insib is-seba' tronġiet mewwija?

—Eh ibni, x'ħaġi hija din li trid taf, qallu dak; kemm ġew u ma reġgħux lura! Iżda inti mur 'il quddiem u ssib ieħor ixjeħ minni u egħref minni; jista' jkun li jgħidlek.

Dak għadda 'l quddiem u mexa ħafna u sa fl-aħħar iltaqa' ma' xiħ ieħor. Malli lemħu qallu:

—Is-sliem għalik, nann!

—Sewwa għamilt, qallu, tgħidli s-sliem għalik, għax kieku ma għidtlix, kont nibilgħek belgħa u nġerrgħek ġergħa.

house and went off along the highroad. Presently he met an old man and said to him:

'Greetings, granddad!'

'You did well to greet me,' the old man answered. 'If you hadn't, I'd have gobbled you up and swallowed you down.'

'Granddad,' the boy went on, 'where can I find the seven citron-maidens?'

'Eh, what a thing that is!' said the old man. 'So many have come and never returned again. But you go straight on until you meet another man, older and wiser than me; maybe he'll tell you.'

The prince started on his way once more, and at last he met another old man. When he spied him he said:

'Greetings, granddad!'

'You did well to greet me,' said the old man. 'If you hadn't, I'd have gobbled you up and swallowed you down.'

'Granddad,' said the boy, 'where can I find the seven citron-maidens?'

'Eh, my boy, what a thing that is you want to know,' said the man. 'So many have come and never returned again. But you push on until you meet another man, older and wiser than me; maybe he'll tell you.'

The prince walked on a long way, and at last he met another man. As soon as he espied him, he said:

'Greetings, granddad!'

'You did well to greet me,' said the old man. 'If you hadn't, I'd have gobbled you up and swallowed you down.'

—Nann, qallu dak, ma tgħidlix fejn insib is-seba' tronġiet mewwija?

—Eħ, qallu x-xiħ, xi trid tagħmel; kemm ġew għalihom u ma reġgħux lura! Inti ismagħni sewwa: imxi 'l quddiem u tara għajn tal-marċa: għidilha: għajn ta' l-ilma żahar, li ma kontx imgħaġġel, kont nieqaf nixrob minnek. Imbagħad tilmaħ siġra tad-dubbien: għidilha: siġra tal-passulina, li ma kontx imgħaġġel, kont niekol minnek. Tara mbagħad kelb irid jiekol it-tiben u ħmar il-għadam: hu il-għadam u tihom lil-kelb, u t-tiben agħtih lil-ħmar; għaddi 'l quddiem u tara lsira sewda tnaddaf il-forn b'idejha: għidilha: xbejba sabiħa, inti b'idejk tiknes il-forn? ħa t-tarf tal-mant tiegħi u naddaf bih. Għaddi 'l quddiem u tilmaħ żewġ ljuni bil-qiegħda mal-ġnieb ta' bieb kbir aħdar; jekk għajnejhom ikunu magħluqin, ter-saqx, għax jikluk; jekk ikunu miftuħin, ersaq, għax il-ljuni jkunu reqdin; mur lejn il-bieb li jħabbat mar-rieħ, agħmillu ħaġra u ħabbat. Tiġi xebba tiftaħ-lek. Malli taraha għidilha: ġejt għas-seba' tronġiet mewwija. Hija tgħidlek: ħalli mmur fuq inġibhom. Inti tistenna xejn, għax ix-xebba tmur biex issinn snienha u tieklok; iżda aħtaf it-tronġiet li huma fuq l-ixkaffa tal-bieb u aħrab bihom għal barra.

Bin is-Sultan għamel dak kollu li qallu x-xiħ.

Meta x-xebba ma sabitx is-seba' tronġiet, ħarġet tiġri barra wara t-tifel u qalet lil-ljuni:

'Granddad,' said the boy, 'won't you tell me where I can find the seven citron-maidens?'

'Eh, what a thing you want to do!' said the old man. 'So many have come for them and never returned again. But listen to me carefully. Walk on, and you'll see a fountain of pus. Say to it, "O fountain of orange-blossom water, if I weren't in such a hurry I'd have stopped to drink of you." Then you'll see a tree of flies. Say to it, "O currant-tree, if I weren't in such a hurry I'd have eaten of you." Then you'll see a dog trying to eat straw, and a donkey trying to eat bones. Take the bones and give them to the dog, and give the straw to the donkey. Pass on farther and you'll see a black slave-girl cleaning an oven with her hands. Say to her, "Fair maiden, is it with your hands you clean the oven? Take the hem of my cloak and clean with it." Walk on again and you'll spy a couple of lions crouching beside a large green gate. If their eyes are shut don't go near them, or they'll eat you up; but if their eyes are open you can come near them, for then the lions will be asleep. Walk up to the gate which is slamming to and fro in the wind, place a stone against it, and knock. A young woman will come and open it. When you see her tell her "I've come for the seven citron-maidens." She'll answer, "Let me go up and fetch them." Don't you wait a second, because the young woman will have only gone in to sharpen her teeth so as to eat you up, but just snatch the citrons which are up on the lintel of the door and run off with them.'

The prince did all that the old man told him.

As soon as the young woman discovered that the

—Aqbduhuli u ibilgħuh!

Il-ljuni qalulha:

—Aħna ma rajniehx la jidħol u lanqas joħroġ.

Ix-xebba dejjem tiġri, qalet lil-lsira:

—Aqbadhuli u ixħtu ġewwa l-forn!

—Le, qaltilha l-lsira, għax huwa qalli: 'xbejba sabiħa' u tani mil-lbies tiegħu biex niknes il-forn!

Ix-xebba qalet lill-kelb:

—Aqbadhuli u igdmu!

—Le, qallha il-kelb, għax huwa biss tani niekol il-għadam u neħħa minn quddiemi t-tiben.

Dik qalet lill-ħmar:

—Mur għalih u agħtih biż-żewġ!

—Le, qallha, għax huwa biss għalifni t-tiben u warrab minn quddiemi l-għadam.

Dik qalet lis-siġra tad-dubbien:

—Inxteħtu għal fuqu, dawwruh u giddmuh!

—Le, qalulha, għax huwa sejjħilna 'siġra tal-passulina,'

Hija f'l-aħħar qalet lill-għajn tal-marċa:

—Għajn, għarrqu ġewwa fik!

—Le, qaltilha il-għajn, għax huwa sejjaħli 'għajn ta' l-ilma żahar!'

U hekk ħadd ma messu u wasal bis-sliema f'lok fejn ma kien hemm ħadd. Waqaf jistrieħ u kiser waħda mis-seba' tronġiet. Malli kisirha ħarġet minnha xebba, qalet: Ġuħ, (bil-ġuħ), ġuħ! għatx, (bil-għatx), għatx! Waqgħet u mietet.

seven citrons were missing she ran out after the youth and said to the lions:

'Seize him and swallow him up!'

'We haven't seen him either going in or coming out,' the lions told her.

The young woman ran on and said to the slave-girl:

'Seize him and shove him in the oven.'

'Oh no!' answered the girl. 'He called me "fair maiden" and gave me some of his clothes to clean the oven with.'

So the woman said to the dog:

'Seize him and bite him!'

'No,' said the dog. 'He was the only one to give me bones to eat and take away the straw.'

She said to the donkey:

'Go after him and give him a good kick!'

'No,' the donkey said. 'He was the only one to give me straw to eat and move away the bones.'

She said to the tree of flies:

'Throw yourselves on him, surround him and bite him to bits!'

'No', they answered her. 'He called us "currant-tree".'

Lastly she said to the fountain of pus:

'Fountain, drown him inside you!'

'No,' said the fountain. 'He called me "Fountain of orange-blossom water".'

So no one touched the prince, and he arrived safely at a place where nobody dwelt. He stopped there to rest, and broke open one of the citrons. As soon as he broke it open a maiden came forth from it, crying:

'Hunger, hungry, hunger! Thirst, thirsty, thirst'! Then she fell down and died.

Kiser tronġa oħra, ħarġet xebba oħra, qalet: Ġuħ, ġuħ! għatx, għatx. Waqgħet u mietet.

Kiser it-tielet, ir-raba', il-ħames u s-sitta u minn kull waħda ħarġet xebba, qalet dawk il-kliem, waqgħet u mietet. Meta ra dan bin is-Sultan qal:

—Dina hija xortija: tlift sitta u ma fadallix ħlief is-seba' waħda; ma għandix nitlef din ukoll.

Għaldaqstant kiseb ikel u xorb, għax kien għoddu wasal id-dar, u meta kiser l-aħħar tronġa u ħarġet ix-xebba u qalet dawk il-kliem, taha tiekol u tixrob.

Ix-xebba ma mititx. Kienet sabiħa daqs ix-xemx u xagħarha kien hekk twil li jiksiha kollha kemm hi, minn fuq rasha sa riġlejha: bil-kemm kienet tidher nitfa minn wiċċha.

—Issa kif sejjer nieħdok hekk, qallha bin is-Sultan, quddiem missieri u ommi minn għajr lbies?

Għax hija barra minn xuxitha, ma kellhiex kisi ieħor.

Għalhekk qallha titla' fuq siġra li kien hemm u tistennieh sa kemm imur iġibilha l-lbies. Hija telgħet fuq is-siġra u huwa telaq għall-palazz.

Issa ħdejn dik is-siġra kien hemm għajn ta' l-ilma li tagħmel għadira fl-art. Ġiet biex timla l-ilma xebba sewda b'qolla f'idha. Malli resqet lejn il-għadira rat fiha xbieha ta' wiċċ ta' mara: ħasbitha tagħha.

—Hi! qalet, u mbagħad jgħidu li jiena kerha u li xuftejja kbar!

16

He broke open another citron, and out came another maiden crying:

'Hunger, hunger! Thirst, thirst!' Then she fell down and died.

He broke open the third, the fourth, the fifth and the sixth, and out came a maiden from each of them, said the same words, then fell down and died. When the prince saw this he said:

'That's just my luck! I've lost six, and now I've only got the seventh left. I mustn't lose it too.'

Thereupon he got some food and drink, for he had almost reached home, and when he broke open the last citron and the maiden came out and said those words, he gave her to eat and drink.

The maiden didn't die. She was as beautiful as the sun, and her hair was so long that it covered her all up, from her head to her feet; scarcely a speck of her face was visible.

'Now however am I going to take you before my father and mother like this, with no clothes on?' said the prince. For she had no covering but her tresses.

So he told her to go up into a tree thereby and wait until he fetched her some clothes. She went up into the tree and he ran off to the palace.

Now near that tree was a spring of water which made a small pool on the ground. A young negress came along with a pitcher in her hand to fill up with water. As soon as she drew near the pool she saw in it the likeness of a woman's face, which she thought was her own.

'Hee!' she said. 'And then people say I'm ugly and my lips are thick!'

Malli qalet dan il-kliem semgħet tifqigħa tad-daħq. Refgħet rasha u lemħet ix-xebba fuq is-siġra. Halliet il-qolla fl-art u qalet lil dik:

—Hallini nitla' ħdejk.

Telgħet, qagħdet ħdejha u qaltilha:

—Hallini niflilek rasek.

Dik ħallietha u qaltilha li hija qiegħda hemm tistenna l-għarus tagħha bil-ħwejjeġ.

—Hi! x'xagħar sabiħ għandek, reġgħet qaltilha is-sewda; u ma' dan il-kliem siltet minn ħobbha splengun u deffsitulha f'rasha kollu kemm hu. Malli daħal f'rasha, ix-xebba saret ħamiema, taret u għabet.

Wara ftit wasal bil-ħwejjeġ bin is-Sultan u malli rafa' rasu għal fuq is-siġra lemaħ is-sewda; baqa' mistagħġeb jħares lejha.

—Kif inti hekk sewda? qallha mill-bogħod.

—Għax domt, weġbitu; ix-xemx ħarqitni.

—X'domt? bil-kemm kelli ż-żmien immur id-dar, u din ma hix fil-bogħod!

L-imsejken infixel aktar u aktar meta resaq u raha sewwa; ma tniffisx aktar, għax qal f'qalbu: Dina xortija!

Ħa immela s-sewda għand missieru u ommu; dawna u kull min raha baqgħu mistagħġbin; imm' issa dik kienet il-għarusa! Għalhekk meta wasal iż-żmien, tejġuhom.

Nhar it-tieġ waqt li kienu mal-mistednin fuq il-

As she said these words she heard a chuckle of laughter. She lifted her head and spied the young woman up in the tree; so she left the pitcher on the ground and said to her:

'Let me come up beside you!'

She went up, sat down beside the maiden and said:

'Let me flea your head!'

She let her do so, and told her that she was sitting there waiting for her fiancé to bring her some clothes.

'Oh, what lovely hair you've got,' the negress kept repeating; and with these words she drew a long pin from her bosom and plunged it right into the maiden's head. When it entered her head the maiden turned into a dove, flew up and vanished.

After a time the king's son came back with the clothes. On looking up into the tree he spied the negress, and stood staring at her in amazement.

'How is it you're so black?' he asked from afar.

'Because you were such a long time,' she answered. 'The sun burnt me.'

'I, a long time? I had hardly time to go home, and that's not far!'

The poor young man grew more and more perplexed when he drew near and had a good look at her; but he didn't utter another sound, simply saying to himself, 'That's just my luck!'

So then he took the negress to his father and mother. They and everyone who saw her were astonished; but anyhow, she was the bride now!

When the time arrived therefore, they married them.

On the wedding-day they were sitting at table to-

mejda u l-għarusa kienet qiegħda ħdejn bin is-Sultan, il-għarus ra u sema' ħamiema tħabbat mat-tieqa. Qal lin-nies tiftaħ it-tieqa u tħalli l-ħamiema tidħol; imma l-għarusa ma riditx. Il-ħamiema dejjem tittajjar u tħabbat u l-għarus sa fl-aħħar ikkmanda jiftħulha. Malli fetħu t-tieqa, il-ħamiema taret għal fuq l-ispalla tal-għarus. Kienet bajda silġ. Il-għarusa tgħidlu Ħalliha! ħalliha! xi tridha? . . . u huwa jżiegħel biha. Waqt li subgħajh kienu jmissulha rasha, ħass fiha ras ta' labra kbira.

—Hi! qal, dan x'inhu li għandha f'rasha?

Silet l-isplengun u l-ħamiema bajda saret ix-xebba li kienet ħarġet minn ġewwa l-aħħar tronġa.

Ix-xebba qaltlu dak kollu li ġralha meta huwa twarrab biex iġibilha l-ħwejjeġ u kif dik is-sewda riedet toqtolha.

Qabdu għaldaqshekk lil dik is-sewda bħala qattiela, telquha f'idejn l-imħallfin, neħħewha, qaxxruha u l-ġild tagħha għamluh ħasira għall-bieb.

U x-xebba tat-tronġa l-mewwija żewġuha lil bin is-Sultan.

U għammru u tammru u spiċċat.

gether with their guests, and the bride was sitting next to the king's son, when the bridegroom saw and heard a dove beating against the window. He told the people to open the window and let the dove in, but the bride didn't want it at all. However, the dove kept flying around and beating against the window until at last the bridegroom ordered it to be opened. When they opened the window the dove flew straight in down on the bridegroom's shoulder. It was as white as snow. The bride kept on saying:

'Leave it alone! Leave it alone! What do you want with it?'

All the while he was stroking it. While his fingers were touching its head, he felt in it the head of a large pin.

'Oh!' he cried. 'What is this in its head?'

He drew out the pin, and the white dove was changed back into the maiden that had come forth from the last citron. The maiden told him all that had happened to her when he went away to fetch her the clothes, and how the negress had tried to kill her.

Thereupon they seized the negress as a murderer. They left her in the hands of the judges, who did away with her. They flayed her, and made her skin into a doormat.

And they married the citron-maiden to the king's son. And they lived many years, and had many children. THE END.

Bin Sajjied

DARBA jkun hemm sajjied u kellu ħamest itfal. U l-iżgħar wieħed minnhom baqa' jmur l-iskola. Meta għalaq l-erbatax-il sena missieru sejjaħlu u qallu: 'Issa tifel bħalek fadallek żmien l-iskola? Ma tarax l'aħna batuti? Għax ma toħroġx, u tiġi magħna ttina daqqa t'id?' U biex ma ntawwalx ħarġu mill-iskola.

L-għada qabel sebaħ mar magħhom jistadu u qabdu awwista kbira. Iż-żgħir ried jeħodha għand is-Sultan imma missieru ma riedx. Qallu: 'Le, ħej, ghax ir-Re jgħidlek grazzi u xejn iktar. U aħna ħuta bħal din 'k inbigħuha naqilgħu l-flus.' Imma ż-żgħir baqa' jitlob biex jeħduha lir-Re u fl-aħħar dawru 'l missieru. U mar biha.

Sab lis-sentinella fil-bieb u qallu għalfejn mar. Daħal, qegħedha fil-baċir u r-Re tant ħa gost biha. Issa t-tifla tar-Re kienet tħares mit-tieqa u meta r-Re taħ borża flus, niżlet waqqfitu huwa u ħiereġ, u qaltlu: 'Ħa borża flus. Imma qis li tmur l-iskola! Trid tmur l-iskola, u jumejn oħra ngħaddi jien nar' intix hemm.'

U sema' minnha. Mar għand is-surmastru. Dan qallu: 'Hawn trid tħallas!' Qallu: 'Mela le!' Reġa'

22

The Fisherman's Son

O NCE there was a fisherman and he had five sons, and the youngest of them was still going to school. When he reached the age of fifteen his father called him and said to him: 'Now has a boy like you still got time left for school? Don't you see we're badly off? Why don't you leave, and come with us to give us a hand?' And not to make a long story of it, he left school.

Next day before dawn he went fishing with them, and they caught a large lobster. The young one wanted to take it to the King, but his father didn't want that. He said to him: 'No, of course not, because the King will just say thank-you to you and nothing more. And if we sell a fish like this we shall make some money.' But the youngster went on begging for them to take it to the King, and in the end he got round his father. And off he went with it.

He found the sentry at the gate and told him why he had come. He went in, put the lobster in a basin, and the King was ever so pleased with it. Now the King's daughter was watching from the window, and when the King gave him a purseful of money she ran down and stopped him just as he was leaving and said to him: 'Take a purseful of money. But promise you will go to school. You must go to school, and in two days' time I'll call and see whether you're there.'

He listened to her, and went to see the teacher. The teacher said to him: 'Here you'll have to pay.' The

qallu: 'Trid tħallas bis-sitt xhur quddiem.' U qallu: 'Iva', u daħal. Poġġieh l-aħħar bank għax kellu erbat itfal mill-aħjar u kien għadu ma jafx x'isarraf. Wara li ħarġu, qallu: 'Inti taf skola?' Qallu: 'Mela le?' Tah jispelli bl-Ingliz u bit-Taljan, u jagħmel is-somom u jikteb, u qal: 'Dan jaf aktar minni!'

Wara jumejn ġiet it-tifla tar-Re tara kif sejjer u qallha tajjeb. Reġgħet ġiet jumejn wara u qalet lis-surmast li kellha grazzja mat-tifel u talbitu jgħid lil missierha. Għall-ewwel ma riedx, imma fl-aħħar mar u qallu lir-Re. U sa flaħħar ir-Re dar u tejjiġhom.

Issa 'l ommu u 'l ħutu ma kien qallhom xejn. Kul- tant kien jara 'l ħutu jbigħu l-ħut. U darba, wara xi sitt xhur, għadda minn quddiem id-dar t'ommu u din għarfitu u qaltlu: 'Kif ħallejtna, ja ħasra! Foqra tant u anqas biss trid taf bina!' Huwa taha għaxar liri u hi ferħet bihom għax rathom dinja. Qatlet ħasi u bagħtet il-forn u ġiebet l-inbid u kielu u xorbu. U hu nesa kollox u dam ma wasal id-dar sal-erbgħa. Meta wasal il-mara bdiet iċċanfru u qaltlu: 'Iwa, hekk timxi miegħi, ja ħabba sajjied l'int! Ma tistħix, sajjied tinten bħalek!' U dak qabad ħwejġu u telaq. Qal:

24

boy said to him: 'Of course I shall.' The teacher told him again: 'You must pay six months in advance.' The boy said to him: 'Yes,' and entered. The teacher put him on the last bench because he had a few very good boys and he didn't know yet what he was worth. When they went out he said to him: 'Do you know how to read?' The boy said to the teacher: 'Of course I do.' He gave him something to spell in English and Italian, some sums to do and something to write, then he said: 'This boy knows more than I do!'

After a couple of days the King's daughter came to see how he was getting on, and the teacher told her very well. She came again two days later and told the teacher that she was in love with the boy, and begged him to tell her father. At first he didn't want to, but in the end he went and told the King. And finally the King came round, and married them.

Now the boy hadn't said anything to his mother and his brothers. Every now and then he used to see his brothers selling fish. And once, after about six months, he passed in front of his mother's house and she recognized him and said to him: 'Alas, how you've deserted us! We're so poor, and you don't even want so much as to know us!' He gave her ten pounds, and she was very happy with them because she thought they were the whole world. She killed a capon and sent it to the bakery and got some wine, and they ate and drank. And he forgot everything, and didn't arrive home until four. When he arrived his wife began to scold him and said to him: 'So, is that how you treat me, you worthless fisherman! Aren't you ashamed, a stinking fisherman like you?' At that he packed his

'Żu', ħa nitlaq. Għajritni sajjied ninten u ħabba sajjied. Ħalliha mela.'

Niżel ix-xatt u siefer 'il bogħod 'il bogħod. Malli
niżel l-art ra x'jaqbad jagħmel. Qagħad fil-bieb ta'
wieħed nutar u dan daħħlu miegħu jikteb għax għall-
ktiba ma kien jiksru ħadd. Kellu żewġ liri kuljum
kemm dam miegħu. U f'kemm ili ngħidlek dan-nutar
far bin-nies. Sema' r-Re ta' dik l-art bih, bagħat
għalih u ħadu miegħu, u lin-nutar ħariġlu erba' liri
kuljum. Mill-ewwel beda ma jitkellimx, iċaqlaq rasu
biss. U r-Re ħareġ il-karti u waħħalhom, li jagħti nofs
miljun lira jekk ifejqulu l-mutu li kellu miegħu. Jekk
le, wara tlitt ijiem jaqtagħlhom rashom. Ġie wieħed
Professur Ġermaniż u m'għamel xejn. Ġew oħrajn u
kollha xorta—qatagħlhom rashom ilkoll!

U fl-art tat-tifla tar-Re, martu, waslet dik il-ktiba
wkoll, u għarfuha li kienet tiegħu. Hi waħħlet f'rasha
li tmur għalih. Libset ta' ġuvni, qatgħet xagħarha, u
siefret. Meta r-Re ta' l-art l-oħra qallha li jekk ma
jirnexxilhiex jaqtagħlha rasha, qaltlu: 'Nindaħal
għaliha din!' Meta kienet miegħu fil-kamra qaltlu:
'Kemm kellek tħabbatni? Kellek ħila ġġibni s'hawn
warajk?' U hu ma tkellem xejn. Kielu u mar jorqod
frisk bħal ħassa. U hi ma raqdet xejn li xejn. Għaddew

things and went off. He said: 'Well, I'd better go. She called me a stinking fisherman and a worthless fisherman. Let her be gone, then!'

He went down to the harbour and sailed far far away. When he landed he looked to see what he could get to do. He sat at the door of a notary and the notary took him in with him as a scribe, because no one could beat him at handwriting. He got two pounds a day as long as he remained with him. In a very short time the notary's clients simply overflowed. The King of that land heard about him, sent for him and took him to work for him, and allowed the notary four pounds every day. From the very first he didn't speak, but just wagged his head. And the King issued posters and had them stuck up, saying he would give half a million pounds if anyone could cure his mute scribe. But if they failed, after three days he would cut off their heads. A German Professor came, but he couldn't do anything. Others came but they were all the same —he cut off all their heads.

The proclamation reached also the country where his wife, the King's daughter, lived, and everyone knew that it was his handwriting. She got it into her head to go after him. She dressed up as a young man, cut off her hair, and sailed. When the King of the other country told her that if she didn't succeed he would cut off her head she said to him: 'I'll go in for this!' When she was with her husband in the room she said to him: 'What a lot of trouble you've given me! You even brought me all this way to look for you.' And he didn't utter a word. They ate, and he went off to sleep as cool as a cucumber. But she didn't sleep a

tlitt ijiem u hu ma tkellemx u sejrin biha għall-mewt.

Is-sajjied tela' ħdejn ir-Re. Qabel ma għallquha, talbet grazzja lir-Re. Malajr qabeż il-mutu qal: 'Jien tifel ta' sajjied! Jien sajjied ninten! Jien ħabba sajjied! Grazzja għandek, barra l-mewt!'

U billi tkellem ma qatluhiex, u reġgħu marru flimkien.

wink. Three days passed, and still he didn't speak, and they were going to take her to be killed.

The fisherman went up beside the King. Before they strung her up, she begged a favour of the King. Suddenly the mute began to say: 'I'm the son of a fisherman! I'm a stinking fisherman! I'm a worthless fisherman! Any favour you like, except not to die!'

And because he spoke they didn't kill her, and they both came together again.

Għanjiet tal-Poplu

1

HANINA sejjer insiefer,
  Ja ħasra ma niħdokx miegħi.
  Lilek Alla jagħtik is-sabar,
  U jżommok fl-imħabba tiegħi.

Iżommok fl-imħabba tiegħi
  Biex dejjem tiftakar fija,
  Iftakar li jien ħabbejtek
  Mindu kont ċkejken tarbija.

Mindu kont ċkejken tarbija
  Qalbi kollha ngibdet lejk;
  Bl-ebda dawl ma nista' nimxi
  Għar bid-dawl tas-sbieħ għajnejk.

Meta niftakar li jiena sejjer,
  Dad-dulur x'jiġini kbir;
  'K Alla jrid, O ħanina,
  Għad tgawdini u ngawdik.

2

O lilek tal-gallerija,
  Idħol ġewwa aħseb dnubietek!
  Ħutek koroh kollha żżewġu,
  Int sabiħa ħadd ma riedek.

Popular Songs

1

My dear, I must go on a long journey;
  Alas, I cannot take you with me.
  I pray God to give you fortitude
  And to keep you fast in my love.

May He keep you fast in my love,
  So that always you think about me:
  Remember that I loved you truly
  Ever since I was a little child.

Ever since I was a little child
  All my heart has been drawn towards you;
  In no other light I can walk
  But the light of your beautiful eyes.

When I think that I go on a journey
  What great sorrow comes upon me!
  If it be God's will, my darling,
  We shall yet rejoice one another.

2

Fair lady up on your balcony,
  Go inside, and think on your sins!
  Your ugly sisters are all married:
  You, the pretty one, no man desired.

3

Demmi ċarċar ġol-għadajjar,
   L-għasafar niżlu xorbuh;
Meta nara l-ħelu wiċċek
   Mn' għajnejja jaqbeż id-dmugħ.

4

Ejja 'l hawn, la tibżax minni,
   Bil-katina ma norbtokx;
Norbtok biss bil-għerq ta' qalbi,
   F'ħajti kollha ma nħollokx.

5

Smajt tisfira f'nofs ta' baħar;
   Kien namur ta' żewġ ħutiet.
Jinnamraw il-ħut fil-baħar,
   Aħseb w ara ix-xebbiet.

6

Dawk għajnejk iħarsu lejja,
   Dak fommok ma jidħaklix:
Donnok trid xi ħaġa minni
   W għall-mistħija ma tgħidlix.

7

Ara x'rajt u x'kelli nara!
   Mara xiħa bil-karkur,
Xuxtha bajdet, snienha waqgħu,
   W għadha tagħmel in-namur!

3

My blood spilled out in the pools,
  The birds came down and drank it;
  When I look on your lovely face
  Ah, the tears spring forth from my eyes.

4

Come you here, don't be afraid of me;
  Not with chains will I bind you fast;
  Only with my heart's cords I'll bind you
  Nor in all my life let you go.

5

In mid-ocean I heard a whistling:
  It was two fishes a-courting.
  The fish in the sea go courting—
  Think, what of the lasses ashore!

6

Your eyes gaze fondly upon me,
  But your lips laugh never at all:
  It's as if you want something of me
  But you're too shy to tell me what.

7

What a thing I've just had to witness!
  An old woman slopping in slippers,
  Her hair white, her teeth all missing,
  Yet still she is going a-courting!

Ħaġa Moħġaġa

IL-BNIEDEM

HAWN ħaġa:
Fil-għodu fuq erbgħa,
F'nofs inhar fuq tnejn,
Fil-għaxija fuq tlieta.

ULIED

WIEĦED u tnejn mhuma xejn,
Tnejn u tlieta logħob u ħlieqa,
Minn tlieta 'l fuq jagħtu bil-buq.

ILSIEN TA' MARA

HAĠA moħġaġa:
Taqta' daqs imqass — imqass mhijiex,
Tniggeż daqs xewka — xewka mhijiex.

IL-WIĊĊ

HAWN ħaġa:
Sittax jaħdmu,
Sittax qegħdin,
Żewġ ragħajja,
Żewġ semmiegħa
U wieħed skantat.

Riddle-me-ree

MAN

HERE'S a thing:
In the morning goes on four,
At midday goes on two,
In the evening goes on three.

CHILDREN

ONE and two aren't very much,
Two and three—playing and joking,
From three upwards—hit with a stick.

A WOMAN'S TONGUE

RIDDLE-ME-REE:
It cuts like scissors, but isn't scissors,
Stings like a thorn, but isn't a thorn.

THE FACE

HERE'S a thing:
Sixteen working,
Sixteen resting,
Two shepherds,
Two listeners,
And one a-stare.

IL-HALQ

Sala b'ħafna siġġijiet,
Pulċinell jiżfen fin-nofs.

IL-QALB

Haġa moħġaġa:
Imsakkra ġo fik
U jistgħu jisirquhielek.

IN-NIFS

Haġa moħġaġa:
Ma tistax iżżommha iktar minn minuta
Għalkemm ħafifa iktar minn rixa.

THE MOUTH

A DRAWING-ROOM with many chairs,
In the middle a clown dancing.

THE HEART

RIDDLE-ME-REE:
Locked up inside you
And yet they can steal it from you.

THE BREATH

RIDDLE-ME-REE:
You cannot hold it more than a minute
Though it is lighter than a feather.

PART TWO

Prose Writings

The End of the Arab Domination in Malta

TIME passed, and the star of the Arabs was beginning to decline over Europe. They were assailed both in Spain and Sicily; they began to suffer defeat and to lose ground everywhere. In Sicily they were attacked by Count Roger, a French lord from Normandy and one of the greatest warriors of his time, with thousands of brave and powerful troops. When the Count had taken possession of the greater part of Sicily and had well under control the Saracens still remaining there, he decided also to deliver our islands out of bondage. The Maltese people had been expecting him for a long time, and an understanding already existed. The Count appeared off Malta with his ships and men in the summer of 1090. He approached the bay which still bears the name of *Miġra l-ferħ*, that is 'the Run of Joy'; for infinitely joyful at his arrival, the Maltese ran to that shore bearing crosses and olive branches to welcome him. The Count landed together with his nobles amid shouts of rejoicing and prayer: the population cried in Greek *Kyrie eleison* which means 'Lord have mercy upon us'. They led him through their main road where the Christians used mostly to meet—*Wied ir-Rum*—a name that has remained, signifying 'The Valley of the Christians'.

Here we would like to quote a few words written on another occasion.

Before Count Roger set siege to Mdina he first went about the island to reconnoitre, and to subdue the Saracens who were scattered here and there. Many of them he drove away, the rest he defeated; this he did so that he would encounter no obstacles when he marched on Mdina. As soon as he was satisfied that the Saracens outside the city would give him no further trouble, and that nothing remained to be done to deliver the island from their yoke but to win over Mdina from them, he went up against it and surrounded it with his men. Since the name of Count Roger brought great terror to the Saracens because he had always defeated them, their commander and all those with him trembled with fear when they beheld themselves shut up inside Mdina, encircled by the Count's soldiers. As the commander saw that the Count was anxious to come to blows without delay, he sent one of his officers to see whether they could come to an agreement. Roger received the delegation but desired that the governor should leave Malta with his men immediately.

This last condition concerning the departure of the governor was not expressed precisely in those words. The agreement between him and the Count was as follows: The governor should surrender the islands and hand over some horses and mules (we do not know how many) together with some munitions of war; he should set free the Christian slaves (they were mostly Sicilians and Spaniards); he could leave Malta and take away with him all his possessions; all who wished to do so could leave with him; but those who wished to remain would pay an annual tribute. The

Count was not hard on the Saracens, and as everyone can see from what we have said, it is not true that he expelled them from our islands; he only took away their rights. It would have been better had he expelled them forthwith, as we shall see presently. The governor sailed to Barbary and many others followed his example, but others remained, content to pay tribute.

When the Count saw that he was now lord of the islands and that he was so well regarded by the Maltese he began to consider how he could place them in the best possible position.

A great part of the walls of Mdina were no longer safe; he therefore gave orders that they should be repaired without loss of time in case trouble should spring up from Tunis. He also built and added to the city a castle which would furnish a first line of defence if ever the city were attacked. The principal church was virtually in ruins; the Count had it repaired and provided for it all that was necessary both inside and out, as regards the building itself and the decoration. There was no bishop; the Count asked the Pope Urban II to appoint as bishop a certain priest named Gualtieri. He also established three canonries, those of archdeacon, dean, and treasurer.

Roger had made very fine laws for Sicily, giving each town its own parliament: he desired that these laws should apply to Malta too, and gave it a parliament also which the Maltese began shortly afterwards to call the 'Popular Council'—formed of persons from every rank and class elected annually by the people. After a time we find the four Magistrates who took care of the provisions of the island as well as other things. All that we have mentioned he did also in Gozo. That which today we call Government was then called *Università*. From what we have said everyone can see that Roger left the islands in the hands of the Maltese themselves, to be governed by their own prudence. We must add that together with the Maltese there were also some Sicilians, for from that time onward Malta and Sicily had become one. The Count left in our islands a Captain with some soldiers who were distributed in the castle of St. Angelo, that of Imdina, and in the Gozo tower, also built by Roger. He gave to the islands the ensign which we rejoice to see to this day on certain festive occasions, white and red.

The coming of Roger to Malta delivered us from people who were, are and will remain our enemies, and the enemies of all those who confess the law and faith of Christ.

Ġ.-A. VASSALLO

The Alarm

ONE spring morning galleys from Tunis appeared unexpectedly off this island. They were many in number and carried thousands of Berbers aboard; for the corsairs had learned to unite and set out on their sweeps in a close formation which rendered them unassailable, and made it easier for them to fall upon the galleys of the Christian princes or to raid towns whenever they could not seize anything on the high seas. Their spoils were then divided among themselves.

All of a sudden the alarm was sounded in our islands. The Dejma who were on guard along the coast set fire to bundles of thorns and made smoke signals: this was a sign that enemy galleys had been sighted on the horizon. The bells of the village churches began to toll loudly; the Constables lost no time in going forth into the village squares to assume command over the people; they sent some men up to the tops of the windmills to sound the harvest-trumpets and call the populace to arms, and they dispatched soldiers into the fields to muster all capable of bearing arms and to warn everybody to gather within the city walls.

A great panic ensued. Everyone abandoned whatever he was doing, hurriedly collected all his possessions and fled towards Mdina or Birġu. The peasants loaded provisions, fodder, and land-produce upon their animals and drove their herds towards the cities, having first hidden such valuables as they could not carry off with them. Some buried chests in their gardens, while some sank boxes in the wells in the hope of recovering them when the Saracens had left and they returned home, if God brought them back safe and sound, for no one knew what would be his luck in the destruction that was about to follow.

The men were confused, the women wept, the children screamed, the animals shied, while the bells tolled on untiringly as if to cry: Flee! Flee!

In a short time the roads were crowded with people and animals, all hurrying towards the cities; fear was on everyone, everyone kept looking back expecting to see the Muslims on their heels. Hearts beat fast, for everyone was afraid that the enemy would fall upon him unawares before he could take refuge behind the walls. Some went on foot, some on horseback, some rode in carriages; those who had room to spare invited others to ride with them; each helped the other as best he could, but nobody lagged on the road.

The sight of those people was pitiful. Children could be seen driving sheep and goats in front of them; youths bent under the weight of bags and baskets; women with babies clutched to their breasts balancing bundles on their heads; men carrying on their backs the aged and the sick who could not walk. Some wept, others cursed the Muslims, others prayed to God to let them off lightly; but everyone hurried along as best he could without even stopping to take breath.

Apart from the Constables, the soldiers of the Dejma, and the men who had taken up arms, no one remained in the villages. These gathered in the square opposite the church, and there, in front of God's house, the Captain delivered a short harangue to encourage them and strengthen their purpose, to defend with their whole hearts their country and their religion; the Constable then made them follow him to meet their fellow soldiers from the other villages as and where it had been prearranged.

When the soldiers had departed, the villages were eerie in the extreme. The bells fell silent, and a great hush, a fearsome silence prevailed. Whereas only a few hours previously life was going on in all its gaiety with the heart-warming laughter and playing of children, while the bustle of people, the sounds of everyday work, the songs of the labourers and the cries of the beasts bore witness to the toil, the industriousness and the unity of the people, and the blessing of God, now everything was deserted; melancholy and terror reigned supreme.

The Saracens did not dally on the sea. In a short time they had landed, and the columns of smoke that suddenly rose from the threshing floors showed that they had lost no time in beginning their work of destruction.

From the bastions of Mdina the people saw the columns of smoke coming nearer and nearer to the city and spreading among the fields of Birkirkara and the meadows of Qormi. They beheld farms flaming like beacons, beasts running in a panic; they heard dogs barking furiously.

Everyone felt his blood freeze, and prayed to God to bring him through the calamity that had befallen them. Meanwhile the gates of Mdina were closed, the drawbridge raised, the soldiers distributed themselves along the bastions and the church-doors opened for the people to place their supplications before God.

Ġ. GALEA

The Ransoming of the Maltese

ONE of the greatest revolutions testifying to the love of the Maltese for their country and their valour was that in which our forefathers ransomed the islands of Malta from the slavery of Monroy's tyranny and that of his Sicilian overlords, and delivered them from the savage Berbers. They were courageous people, and aflame with ardent love for their faith. The Berbers had conquered the shores of North Africa and taken to piracy throughout the Mediterranean. Now they were threatening our islands. In the opinion of many writers, the wonders performed by the Maltese in those days outshine even those of the Great Siege itself.

On 27 November 1399, with the consent of the Sicilian parliament, the islands of Malta were united to the Spanish crown by King Martin. Before, they had occasionally been given as a fief to some count or marquis, under whom our forefathers had suffered much. After a time however, as King Alfonso of Spain was short of money on account of the wars he pawned the Maltese islands to Don Anton Cardona, Viceroy of Sicily, at a price of 30,000 florins, instituting him as governor over them. The latter took an oath that under his rule no injury should be done to the customs and privileges of the people. But when his successor Monroy acted contrary to what Cardona had sworn, the Maltese and the Gozitans took it very ill and rebelled against him. They seized the government of the islands into their own hands and broke out into acts of violence and fury without sparing anyone. A Maltese delegation was sent to Sicily to reach an agreement on the following terms: that the Maltese would repay, in the space of four months, the 30,000 florins for which Monroy had bought the islands, and that pardon should be granted to those who had taken part in the revolt. But when the Maltese delegation returned to Malta the Viceroy of Sicily broke his word, and demanded that the sum should be paid in a much shorter time. The Maltese were infuriated against their Sicilian overlords and revolted against them even more fiercely than before. In those days the greater part of the Maltese population was made up of peasants, and it was they who reacted and put their shoulders to the destruction of their Sicilian lords and the routing of the Berbers.

No one can read this sad story without feeling his heart bleed for the suffering and servitude endured by our forefathers in those days, still called the days of tyranny. The rich were burdened with taxes; the peasants stripped of their very clothes, robbed of their work in the fields to pay the debts of their cruel and greedy lords; the priests were beaten and cast into prison; girls and women were kidnapped and kept as slaves in the palaces of the Sicilian and Spanish grandees. Sobs and prayers were all that the anguished hearts of the Maltese could utter: a cry of pity and patience to God, curses and anger for the enemy that had come to the point of sucking the very blood of the starving Maltese. All around one could behold only misery, hunger, weeping. A veil of melancholy was spread over the whole island; the oppression of the Maltese had actually surpassed that of God's people in the land of Babylon and on Egypt's shores. After a number of petitions which were never accepted, after much patience that proved of no avail, the peasants revolted and with those very tools with which they earned their living and that of their children they routed Monroy's soldiers and slew the overlords who were oppressing them.

In all this turmoil the Berbers, about 18,000 in number, attacked Malta and succeeded in landing at St. Paul's Bay. They came over Mellieħa, mowing down, laying waste, and destroying wherever they passed and leaving behind them masses of dead men and animals and ruined houses, devastation, and burning fields and trees. With shining blades and firearms in their hands they terrified the farmers who gathered at Mosta to obstruct the enemy's way, ready to die as martyrs for the ransoming of Malta and for the Cross of Christ, rather than fall as slaves to the enemies of Christendom.

Flashes of fire appeared from the bastions and from the terraces of houses. A huge mass of flames reddened the skies and the seas over and around the island. But all of a sudden, after three days of hard fighting and much bloodshed, out of the midst of the smoking tongues of fire was heard sounding the shout of victory of the peasants on the walls of Mdina.

With Monroy's tyrants slain, the Berbers defeated and routed, the ransoming of Malta was now complete under the shadow of the Holy Cross.

REV. B. GRECH, O.F.M.

The Great Victory

THE Great Siege! I suppose there is not one of the historians who have written on the sixteenth century who does not place the great siege of Malta among the finest and greatest events of those hundred years.

Bosio, the historian of the Order who wrote down the history of the siege in all its details, and in his writings prepared the material for all subsequent historians, becoming the most reliable authority on the subject, never tires of showering praises upon Malta's defence during the four months of the Siege.

Scipione Ammirato, put by Samminiatelli Zabarella in the very forefront of his book on our Siege, has this to say in his *Stories of Florence*: 'If, when weighing the facts according to their worth, we do not allow ourselves to be blinded by deceptive appearances, we are able to maintain with all right and truth that the famous battles of Salamis and Marathon—the finest and greatest passages in Greek history—may well pale into insignificance before the defence of Malta.'

That is true glory; that is undying glory.

But if glory is not engendered and does not grow save in lands of lofty ideals, of an iron will, of worthy and valiant deeds, then what were the events which gave to our country the title to this glory? What part did it play in this defence? What did it perform, what was its worth, what did it sacrifice of its treasure, its strength, its health, its life, that 8 September 1565 should have become what it is today, a date written in letters of gold in the history of the Christian religion and of European civilization?

Listen to the facts, which would have sounded like a legend ornamented by the imagination of some poet, did they not belong to real history, supported by contemporary documents which nobody can contest.

At dawn on 18 May 1565 there echoed over Malta three cannon shots from the forts of St. Angelo, St. Elmo, and St. Michael. This was the strong voice of a mother, of our country calling her sons, our forefathers, to drop their tools of toil and take up the weapons of war.

The Turkish fleet, the most powerful of those times, charged with that army whose very name made monarchs tremble, armed with the most recent instruments of war and with all that the art of warfare demanded, besides whatever was required by the evil desires and powerful mind of Sultan Soliman, who had sworn that he would sweep the Knights of St. John out of Malta, had appeared in unending columns on the pale horizon, advancing with billowing sails towards this dear little island which is our homeland.

The summons worked like magic. Inside the cities the knights made themselves ready in a flash. In the country Maltese of every class in every part of the island looked once about them; they understood; they left their work just as it was, let go of their tools and an hour later appeared in bands with weapons in their hands marching towards the city to see what was afoot and to receive their due orders.

The young people and the womenfolk stayed behind

to collect from the fields and out of the villages all that could serve as sustenance for the soldiers and fodder for the animals. After two days, placed at their posts by the experienced mind of a wise and valorous Knight, having a strong hope in God and hearts of lions in their breasts, they were ready and waiting for the foe to do battle with him, having sworn to conquer or to die.

Alas, how few were their numbers! For every one of them there were four of the enemy! But Heaven was on their side, and this they believed firmly.

One hundred and eleven times the sun rose and set, and every day it looked sadly down out of a smoke-laden sky upon the fearful battle which went on unremittingly, without any respite, without any mercy; upon flames of fire that flashed out of the mouths of the savage cannons; upon a hail of cannon balls, of stones, of arrows; upon a network of gleaming sabres; upon terrifying scenes of hacking, cleaving, rending, groaning, of pain, sobbing, bereavement, sorrow, destruction, tears, blood, and death; while Europe looked on fearful and amazed, waiting—alas, somewhat listlessly—to see the end of the struggle.

Our men were in the right; and hope did not deceive them. St. Elmo, St. Michael, and the Castille opened up like three fearful tombs, and numberless were the Muslims who vanished inside them.

At dawn of 8 September the church bells rang solemnly; from the shattered bastions cannon were fired; from ruined houses, from clean-swept fields issued a sigh of repose; from the crowded squares the thunderous cry of victory was heard, and from the church of St. Lawrence of Birġu, in joyous albeit tearful voices, a hymn of thanksgiving to God and to the Child Mary spread abroad through the moist morning air. From that day forward, the day of victory was linked so inseparably with the feast-day commemorating the Virgin's birth that the word Vittorja in our country came to denote both the one and the other.

The army of Soliman the terror of Europe, broken, routed, with three men lost out of every four, loaded with shame and disgrace embarked once more in the galleys, impoverished of sailors and oarsmen, and like a lean, dazed man slowly moved farther and farther away and vanished, never to reappear.

These were the facts, and this was the victory which robed our island in immortal glory, setting it in so high esteem in the eyes of the whole world. For the fierce struggle which ended in the victory of 8 September was not merely a struggle between the island of Malta with its knights, and Soliman who had come with his immense fleet and army to subdue it, to scorn and humiliate it; it was a struggle, a struggle once and for ever, between the Religion and the Church of Christ on the one hand and the Superstitions of Mahomet and the Muslim Alliance on the other; it was a battle, a decisive battle, between European civilization, the outcome of centuries of deep thought, hard work, and sound discrimination, and the idle, sensual apathy of Mohammedanism which corrupts everything, defiles and destroys everything that does not correspond with its ideas and desires.

The tight hold kept by the galleys of Malta upon

the galleys of Soliman; the capture of the *Sultana* loaded with treasures from the orient, and the tears and imprecations of the harem women who shared in the cargo of that splendid vessel, may well have served to add fuel to the fire; but the roots of the war were much older and went far deeper into the heart of Soliman. Rhodes and Malta should have constituted the opening and the close of the history of his reign. He intended to sweep the knights out of Malta and to make this island a centre of his power in the Mediterranean; he would seize the coasts and from there penetrate deeper into the heart of Europe until he brought all the States under his rule and the laws of Mahomet. This was his dream, and this was the intention of this Sultan, as cruel and terrible as he was powerful and shrewd.

We know what happened during and after the Siege: we know in what state the Turkish fleet left Malta; we know how the captains of the fleet and of the army were received by Soliman. We know that after the battering it received in Malta the Ottoman Power took another beating around the walls of Vienna, and was finished after the mortal blow in the sea of Lepanto. We know too that the Christian religion from its centre in Rome marched tranquilly forward on its triumphant way, and we know that the States of Europe passed on from victory to victory along the path of progress and civilization. But what we do not know, what no power of the imagination can ever discover, is what would have happened if things had not turned out as they did. We can say with all truth, however, that the happenings under the walls of Vienna and in the waters of Lepanto would not have taken the course they actually took: and I know not who could have delivered Italy, and with Italy the heartlands of Europe, from the whirlwind of Soliman's numerous and ruthless army.

Great therefore is the glory that robed our fatherland on 8 September 1565; great, therefore, is Malta's right to the gratitude of all civilized nations.

DUN KARM

Dun Mikiel Xerri

THEN as Dun Mikiel was considered one of the most learned men in Malta and was held by all in the highest esteem, General Vaubois was sincerely desirous of releasing him, and when he was brought into court for the hearing of his case the general came in person to question him according to the requirements of the law. He wanted him to say something or other which would enable him to moderate the charge, but the great French general knew not how much greater than himself the little Maltese priest was, both in courage and manliness.

'Professor Xerri,' he said to him with complete composure and calmness, to show him that he was not offended against him so much as against the others, 'you know you have been brought before me because, as is alleged, you were implicated in the conspiracy concocted by Guliermu Lorenzi against us, and played an important part in it.'

'Yes . . .'

'You are also aware that such offences in time of war, as we find ourselves at present, are punished by death.'

'Yes . . .'

'Now, Professor, understand me clearly: if you would like some time to think the matter over well before answering me, I can grant you it.'

'No . . .'

'You don't want any time?'

'No . . .'

General Vaubois let fall on the table the paper he held in his hands containing the names of the accused; he held back his words as if terrified by the question he was about to put and for a while gazed fixedly at Dun Mikiel who was standing in front of him in the middle of the chamber, wearing his soutane and holding a breviary in his hands.

At that moment the Master, standing all alone between the row of generals all wearing their plumed hats and spread along the table in front of him and the row of the accused who were held back by the soldiers a few paces behind him, looked a very angel of power! The two sergeants who flanked him on either side with drawn swords began to tremble in his stead. . . . Dun Mikiel himself had never trembled in his life, except when kneeling down before the God who made him. . . .

'What do you wish to say then?'

'Guilty.'

'Did you take part in the conspiracy?'

'I did . . .'

'An important part?'

'Yes . . .'

'All these others, were they all with you?'

The Master crossed his arms on his breast, lowered his head and answered not a word.

It was a moment of fear. The generals gazed open-mouthed in amazement at the man. The soldiers envied him and wished that they had his courage. The accused were terrified.

'Do you not answer?'

'I would like to ask you a question first, great General of France.'

'You have a perfect right to do so.'

'Did you summon me before you to confess my crimes, or to stain my honour?'

Vaubois was on the verge of taking offence; but as he had a fixed idea in his head—to make him name some other people so that he might let him off lightly —he kept a tight rein on his tongue and continued:

'Whoever tells the truth does his duty, and we do not want to hear anything from you but the whole truth . . .'

'I shall tell you the truth about myself; the truth about others you must find out for yourselves. Since you know how to discover them, go and knock on other doors.'

'What is the truth about yourself?' asked Major Boudard who was sitting at the end of the table, his blood boiling at all that cossetting on General Vaubois' part.

'That I am guilty since I took an important part in the conspiracy . . . that I desired with all my heart that it might succeed . . . that I do not wish to defend myself before you . . . that there is only one thing I regret . . .'

'What thing? What do you regret?' cried the judges who had all risen to their feet with anger in their faces.

'That we trusted ourselves to the hands of a foreigner . . . that I did not take charge of the whole affair myself . . . that we were not in time to deliver the four cities from your yoke . . .'

He hurriedly made the sign of the cross, folded his arms again on his breast, and lowered his head.

'Take him out till we write the sentence,' said Vaubois at last, thoroughly enraged.

'And the others?' asked his adjutant.

'Remove them as well. There's no need for us to hear the evidence in their presence; after all, thirty-three of them we caught red-handed and the others haven't opened their mouths to plead not guilty. Take them away quickly.'

This, as everyone knows, was the 16th of January in the afternoon. After one hour or a little less Major Boudard, his face flushed with the rage he was in, went down to the prison with a paper in his hand accompanied by two soldiers. He called the prisoners out of their cells, ordered the soldiers to put them in a row in front of him and read out to them the sentence of the Council of War.

'They will all be shot in the middle of the Palace Square at Valletta under the Staff of Liberty, Professor Xerri and twelve of his companions within twenty-four hours, the rest in daily batches.'

It is known from the parish registers preserved in the churches of St. Paul and St. Dominic that Mattew Pulis lost his life for his country on 29 January, that Wiġi Damatu dragged on until 11 February, that Ċensu Dimek (perhaps because they hoped to get something out of him) was not shot till seventy days later, on 27 March.

It must not be thought that Dun Mikiel was distressed. The others were afraid since everyone fears death, especially the twelve chosen without warning to die on the morrow; but he feared nothing. As the Major walked away and the soldiers led him once more to his cell, Dun Mikiel slowly made the sign of the cross, put on his spectacles, opened his breviary between his two hands and began to recite the office, standing in the middle of the cell beneath the glimmer of light that hung from the ceiling.

Then after about an hour, when he had said the office to the last word, he asked the sergeant who had remained shut up with him for a pen and an inkpot and left in writing all his books to the Mdina Seminary. He crossed himself again, removed his spectacles and stretched out on the mattress thrown down in the corner of the cell.

He spoke no more till the next morning, but a little after dawn he received a visit which far from distressing him filled him with courage. It was Bishop Labini who by leave of General Vaubois came in to him, his face pale as death and with tears in his eyes.

'Dun Mikiel, I wish I could have brought you good news but I couldn't do anything . . . They said you behaved very badly with them.'

'I behaved like a man, as with God's help I shall do to the last. I ask for only one favour, if you can obtain it for me . . .'

'Tell me, tell me . . .'

'I desire to be the last to be shot so that I can assist the others and do my duty to them.'

'Nothing more?'

'Nothing, except your blessing.'

And he knelt down in front of him with all reverence, as if to kiss his hand before saying Mass.

Labini could stand it no longer. Beside that heart of a lion he felt his own heart as small as a lamb's, and as soon as he had blessed him he ran out of the cell crying and sobbing like a child. . . .

But Dun Mikiel was not disturbed in the least; he pitied that poor man who, because of his goodness, was suffering so much at the hands of the French. Now that he remained alone in his cell with the sergeant on guard he began once more to recite the office for the day.

All of a sudden a great uproar could be heard. Cries of joy! The rolling of drums and clashing of swords and muskets! Laughter and cursing of many people who seemed drunk with joy. . . .

It was Bonaparte's soldiers going to fetch the thirteen Maltese whom they were to shoot that dawn.

They took them out two by two from the prison of St. Elmo and led them to the Square, sometimes pushing them from behind and at other times dragging them by their arms amid the barking of dogs, the cursing of sergeants, the rejoicing of all the traitors, among whom there were a few Maltese and many Frenchmen, not because the condemned men resisted or could not walk but because those children of the New Liberty wanted to make a carnival out of them. Poor liberty of France! Thus it was born, and thus it has remained.

Dun Mikiel, still wearing his soutane, with a small crucifix in one hand and the breviary in the other was walking in the middle of a squad of soldiers, steady and erect like the Statue of Manhood advancing to reprimand such childish and shameful behaviour.

Among the twelve who were to be executed were
Lieutenant Peralta and Dun Miju ta' Nurata who
remained courageous to the last. But some of the
others who, as is known, were simple country folk
started growing pale and trembling when they found
themselves in the middle of the Square surrounded
by rows of soldiers, some of whom had already begun
to load their muskets to shoot them. But Dun Mikiel
suddenly rushed up to them with the crucifix held on
high, as if he were not one of those to be executed.

'Now is the time', he told them, 'to show the world
what Malta is worth! Let us shed our blood for our
country with a stout heart, that God may have mercy
on our souls. Look at Jesus who died without fault
for our faults. . . . Brethren, let us repent of our
sins. . . .'

And still holding high his crucifix he knelt down
so that the others might do likewise.

Then, when the sergeants came up to them to
blindfold them and had covered the eyes of all the
others, one of them went up to Dun Mikiel with a
cloth in his hand.

'No, not me,' he said in a low voice so that the rest
might not hear him. 'No, not me. I do not need to hide
my face to die for my country.'

And he took out his spectacles from his pocket,
fixed them before his eyes and stared at the soldiers
who were taking aim.

Lastly he took his watch from his waistcoat pocket
and gave it to the sergeant.

'Soldier of France,' he addressed him again, 'this
is for you, to tell them to shoot me in the heart.'

He kissed the cross, folded his arms on his breast, stared the soldiers in the face and shouted in a loud voice that echoed around the whole square.

'Long live Malta! God be with us! Fire!'

At that word a salvo of muskets barked, and thirteen corpses fell to the ground—thirteen men who gave their lives for the honour and love of their country: thirteen martyrs.

Ġ. MUSCAT-AZZOPARDI

Vassalli and His Work

ALTHOUGH the road opened for us by Vassalli was destined in all justice to lead to the goal those workers who succeeded him in the field of Maltese writing, we cannot say, this century and more after his death, that it was entirely smooth. On the contrary, those same obstacles which the Father of Maltese Writing encountered and experienced, through the bitter and harsh resistance of the enemies of the Maltese language, also held back the few workers who came after him; so fierce indeed was that resistance, that there were times when they were discouraged, lost all enthusiasm, and let their work be buried under the heap of stones flung at them.

In Vassalli, however, we witness the strength of mind of a man who kept on working to his last breath despite the fact that, by the irony of fate, under the scourge of envy and hatred prompted by political considerations inimical to those ideals of national democracy which burned within his young heart, he had for more than thirty years to suffer imprisonment, exile from his country, and afterwards, together with his children, hunger and poverty, finally to die ridiculed and destitute and to be buried in a grave over which the compassionate hand of those who appreciated him was even afraid to engrave his name.

One of the faults for which Vassalli is always blamed is that his grammatical system, from the alphabet onwards, was built on foundations that were theoretical rather than practical and for this reason found no one to accept it; it thus remained as it were a mere document of philological interest without any usefulness for the education of the people. We must acknowledge however that in his time the grammatical study of the languages, especially of Maltese whose grammar was still in the making, was planned on minute rules instead of that practical sense which is acquired gradually through the actual use of the language in literary writing. But even more than Vassalli's hard-headedness in being too much attached to the etymological and grammatical rules of the Semitic languages, even more than the lack of a practical sense which he might have had, what did most to ruin and kill Vassalli's system and consequently to bring death upon the nascent Maltese writing, which had to wait over a hundred years to see the light of a new life, were the circumstances and the times in which Vassalli lived. And if today we can say that Maltese has come to life once more and again raised its head and entered into the share and rights of those languages which are taught, written, and adorned with something of a literature, we can say without any shame or hesitation that beside the enthusiasm, effort, and patience of people who in the last forty years did not shrink from passing along the path which had once been opened for them by Vassalli and continuing along the road till they reached the end, beside the courageous and useful work of these people, we must confess that it was also due to the times and circumstances that Maltese waxed strong and grew in its young written literature.

We can say that but for the times and circumstances, Vassalli's name would not today have to be cleansed of the second disgrace on account of which many of the children of Malta in present times still pull a long face at the mention of his name; we need make no mention of the first disgrace, that sin which until recently educated people saw in Vassalli's effort to found the writing of Maltese. Today his name has redeemed itself of this disgrace quite naturally because time has rendered *justice* to his ideas. Vassalli was born too early for his work to have the necessary help and for his ideas to be consolidated. His were times when all learning as such was founded on the classical Latin school; in those days no one would dream of studying the vernacular tongues of tiny countries such as Malta, although scholars did not disdain to do so. Maltese could then be fitted into some corner of scholarship as a branch of academic exercise, that is to say as one tiny link among the many that make up the chain of ancient oriental languages which, in those days, had begun to be studied by European scholars and especially at the Propaganda Fide in Rome.

Vassalli's first Maltese grammar was written in Latin, the language of scholars in his time, just as Latin had also been used by those who, some years before him, had written about Maltese as a Phoenician-Punic or Carthaginian language, among them Arrigo Maio and Bellermann. For this reason, Vassalli thought that in his lexicon he would introduce Latin as well as Italian for the interpretation of every word.

It was at the beginning of the nineteenth century that Vassalli for more practical reasons, which at that time had already begun to be felt, published his Maltese grammar written in Italian, which was still the only language in which such a learned work could be composed to be of some utility to the students of the country. From that time onwards, little by little there was a growing necessity for Maltese to enter and be disseminated in devotional books; then, along with English it crept into some schools, where very often, for fear that it might prove the ruin of Italian, it was again removed and discarded from the school-books, over and above the apprehension that its alphabet might stand in the way of reading other languages which differed from it, and that its study was of no use at all but rather a waste of time.

Now that today the time has arrived for Maltese to come to stay in our schools, with the hope that as time goes on its teaching will become confirmed in its acquired right as the language of the Maltese people, now that for constitutional, municipal, literary, and national reasons, whether practical or not, we have at last felt the need for Maltese as the tongue of the people to be introduced into the law-courts, the administration and the schools, it is impossible not to bring back before our eyes the image of Vassalli, with all that he went through and all that he did in the service of Maltese. And our thoughts turn naturally to that 'Call to the Maltese Nation' which he made in the introduction of his lexicon published in 1796 where, after having affirmed that his first thought was that his work should serve the good of his native country, after stressing his belief in the utility of teaching Maltese, after declaring that he scorned the criticism of those people who, without sufficient enlightenment and without sufficient training in Maltese but moved by envy, hatred, or other intentions, had tried from the very beginning to thwart his solid work and make him lose hope by means of their contemptuous attitude, he finally explained that although that dictionary, his first enterprise which necessitated careful research, might have certain defects in the explanation of some words, he nevertheless hoped that it would be useful not only to the Maltese of his own time but to those Maltese who would come long after him.

Today Vassalli's dream appears to have almost come true; however, for it to be realized in its entirety it will be necessary for us before all things not to forget that these are not Vassalli's times, when Maltese could pass as an academic study and nothing more, and therefore we must take into consideration that in the teaching of Maltese in elementary and secondary schools, and even at the University, we must conform with the needs of the times: it must be the teaching of writing, of grammar, and of Maltese literature for its own sake, without relation to the study of other sister languages which today, either because they are dead or because they possess only a literary character that is entirely oriental, cannot give to the teaching of Maltese anything but an academic semblance without the least literary or practical value to our country—a thing which may prove of more harm than good.

Above all, three things are necessary: Vassalli's good intentions, brains that resemble his, but also a practical sense greater than that which he possessed.

A. CREMONA

Dun Karm as Poet

As Dun Karm's poems have for many years been scattered in literary and religious periodicals, Dr. G. Bonnici, one of our best novelists and founder, together with Dr. R. Briffa, of the Għaqda tal-Malti (University), could not have done a more useful thing for the benefit of our language than when he collected all these poems into three books, printed on excellent paper. Before this our poet was already known and loved for the beauty of his fine poetry, but now the reader can enjoy much better the sweet flavour of Maltese song. These three volumes certainly merit the handsome title of *Ġnien tal-Poeżija Maltija* ('Garden of Maltese Poetry'), for in them our native Muse revealed herself at her best; she demonstrated the power of the Maltese speech, its beauty, and its ability to soar when well fashioned, as well as the falseness of the ugly rumours spread by the enemies of the Maltese language, that our tongue can never attain the peak of really great poetry. Dun Karm has shown how right Professor A. Cuschieri was when he asked reproachfully:

> Who said that it is heavy and crawls
> Like a snake creeping on its belly?
> See, how light it is,
> How suddenly it leaps and soars.

Dun Karm more than any other writer showed the

Maltese that the tool was sound, and that all that was lacking was a master-craftsman skilled and of good will. The same Carmelite poet Cuschieri reveals to us the secret of Dun Karm's art and shows us why, in his hand, Maltese was no longer that ponderous language, lacking all colour and elegance, which had caused many people to be ashamed of it. Indeed the forceful lines of that 'Poet of the Maltese Word' might very well refer to Dun Karm himself.

> As in his forge the smith
> First of all heats the iron,
> Then little by little works it
> Till it takes the shape he desires,

> So from my hand the word
> I let not go carelessly,
> Like one who hurls a stone
> Not knowing where it will fall.

> But before, I soften it
> In my mind like to a paste,
> Then slowly and patiently
> I give it shape and beauty.

Of a truth the perfect command of the Maltese language, the subtle ability to shape and chisel it into sweet and powerful verses—these constitute the greatest merit of our national poet, and no small merit at that.

When I was still a young man in my twenties, I too was so greatly impressed by the skill of our poet that I wrote the following verses in English.

To him that builds the rhyming of our song
With interwoven music of rich sounds,
That are the herald triumph of our race,
I wish that I could fashion a great hymn,
Pindaric in its flight. The hard-trod glebe,
Whereon the wheat grows not, unploughed, unsown,
Is not more stubborn than our ancient tongue
In its unsoftened power still untamed
By Art's refining breath. But lo! our Singer
Hath hammered out from this time-sacred tongue
The full-toned harmony of abiding joy.

In his lecture *English Catholic Literature* Cardinal
Newman says regarding the beginnings of literatures:
'The language of a nation is at first rude and clumsy;
and it demands a succession of skilful artists to make it
malleable and ductile, and to work it up to its proper
function. It improves by use, but it is not everyone
who can use it while as yet it is unformed. To do this
is an effort of genius; and so men of a peculiar talent
arise, one after another, according to the circumstances
of the times, and accomplish it.'

That is Dun Karm's greatest merit, among others
also great, in relation to Maltese literature. That is the
clearest testimony which Dr. Bonnini's three volumes,
published in 1939, render to the poet. These three
volumes will always be looked upon as the ornament
of every Maltese library.

Before passing on to study Dun Karm's literary
tendencies it will be convenient to learn something of
his life and activities; convenient, because poetry is
like a mirror that reflects a whole sequence of events,
or at least those throughout the life of a poet which

74

made the deepest impression on him. For a poet responds to the murmurings of the heart, which in its turn responds to the joys and sorrows of life. This is a truth which it would be well for some young people to realize. I refer especially to those youths who write poetry without ever having experienced within themselves the tempestuous winds of emotion, and who therefore imagine poetry to be merely the skill of weaving verses and stringing rhymes together. Dun Karm is a poet not because he wrote verses, but because his verses are poetical; and his verses are reckoned poetical not because they are modelled on poetic forms, but because they are inspired. Otherwise his stanzas would have been dead—a body without any spirit.

Dun Karm was born at Żebbuġ on 18 October 1871, that small town which he himself describes in a poem named after it.

The village that would never stand any nuisance,
The village whose blood is the blood of Vassalli and
    Dun Mikiel.

His father Filippu, also from Żebbuġ, spent practically the whole of his life of sixty-two years sailing between Malta, Greece, and the surrounding islands as a businessman, while his mother Lunzjata, whom the poet never forgot even in his old age, was a homely woman from the same town. At the age of six Dun Karm entered the Government school where he remained until he was thirteen. Then in 1884 he joined the Seminary to study for the priesthood. From 1888 to 1890 he studied philosophy, and from 1890 to

1894 he completed his theological course. He was only twenty-two years and seven months old when he was ordained priest on 17 May 1894.

In February of the year following his ordination he was appointed teacher at the Floriana Seminary. During that period Dun Karm began to experience the worst threat to his health, a nervous debility which did not permit him to work as hard as he would have wished. It was a kind of breakdown that is often the result of overstudy, or of some other mental disturbance. To commemorate his recovery from that severe breakdown he wrote a poem in Italian called *Risveglio*, and in his poem *Il-Ġerrejja u Jien* he recalls this terrible attack of neurasthenia in the following lines.

> I struggled and battled
> with billows and whirlwinds,
> and twice I saw Death with her obscene grin
> beckoning me under the waters.

In a letter to me, printed in the first volume of *Ward ta' Qari Malti*, page 191, the poet explains these lines thus. 'When I wrote these verses I recalled—and it was as if a darkness covered my eyes—the severe breakdown which I suffered, a sour and bitter fruit of my imprudent and uncontrolled concentration on books during the last years of my course at the Seminary: a terrible illness which brought me to the edge of the grave, and left me tottering there for many months.'

Concerning his recovery, about which he sang in his Italian poem *Risveglio*, he writes: 'I recalled my recovery; the first days when my blood-stream began to receive strength again and the hope of a new life smiled on me once more; I remembered the ardour and enthusiasm with which I went about my work in my room at the Seminary where I had been called to teach in 1895, and the sweet verses which gushed out of my heart incessantly like a fountain.'

He taught at the Seminary for about twenty-six years, sometimes one subject and sometimes another. He taught Italian, Latin, English, arithmetic, geography, cosmography, Italian literature and Church history together with Christian archaeology for the theological students.

On 1 June 1921, one day after he had given his last lesson in the Seminary, he was appointed Assistant Director of the Public Library, in 1923 Director of Circulating Libraries and university examiner in Italian for matriculation, academic and preparatory courses, and from 1939 onwards also examiner in Maltese for the same courses. He retained the post of Assistant Director of the Public Library until 1936 when he retired on pension. He was then commissioned by the Government to complete the official English–Maltese dictionary which had been begun in 1935 under Dr. Laferla, and on which he made such good progress that the Government printing office could hardly keep up with his work. On 1 October 1945 the Royal University conferred upon him an Honorary D.Litt., he being the first ever to receive that distinction. On 4 August 1946, the day on which Chevalier Ġuże' Muscat-Azzopardi died, he received the gold medal bearing that name and instituted by his friend's son Gino from the hands of the Governor, Francis Campbell Ross Douglas, at a delightful ceremony in the University.

Dun Karm during his life experienced both joy and sorrow. His happiest time was at the Seminary, where he lived among and was befriended by his books, his students and his priest-friends. Once, however, a period of great sorrow and grief invaded this happy life; that was when Cardinal La Fontaine came to Malta as Apostolic Visitor and made some radical changes through which Dun Karm suffered undeservedly. He was sad because he had to separate himself from the Seminary, from teaching, from his students and the other priests. In his letter mentioned above, explaining his autobiographical poem *Il-Ġerrejja u Jien*, he speaks of this time as follows.

I recalled . . . but here my mind wanted to run away, to run away from that dreadful vision. I recalled the times when certain persons with neither heart nor reason, full of themselves and with envy, as well as certain other persons who should have had a little more understanding of their mission, brought about change and damage, and I found myself all alone in consequence. My mother had died a short time before, and I was far away from my brothers and my friends, buried alive inside three tiny rooms in Valletta where I knew nobody and nobody knew me; I had no other companion to share my sadness apart from a small golden bird that brought me what comfort he could with the song I had taught him. This was the second time that I found myself at the grave's edge, and I would have fallen in had I not possessed the hard fibre, steel nerves and firm courage that my father and mother, both strong people of old stock, had given me.

A witness of this period of sadness is the poem *Lil-Kanarin Tiegħi*, full of old memories of the anguish through which he had passed and of the grief he bore all alone in the silence of his room.

> What brought us together in this so silent house
> You perchance do not know, O golden bird;
> Neither do you know why, when I go out
> To my work in the morning, I close the door after me
> And lock it with a key, and never a footstep,
> Never a breath you hear till once again
> I turn the key in the lock, and enter the room.
> Better it is you know not; thus no share
> You take in my sorrow, and between days and nights
> You pass your life without any grief at all.

Dun Karm's literary career can be divided into two periods—the first, during which he wrote poetry in Italian and therefore received from the contemporary Maltese intelligentsia all the praise and glory due to him, and the second, when he gave up writing Italian poetry to compose verses in Maltese. This second period can also be divided into two parts: the time when Maltese was spurned underfoot in its own home in favour of Italian, which consequently brought Dun Karm many enemies, and the better period when Italian surrendered its status of official language to Maltese—which had every right to be the ruling language in the very home of the people who spoke it.

Let us consider the first period of our poet, the period during which Dun Karm wrote in Italian. In 1896, when he was only twenty-five, he collected all the poems he had written from the age of seventeen to twenty-four, the time when all things glitter before our phantasy, the time about which Keats wrote in his introduction to *Endymion*: 'The imagination of the boy is healthy, and the mature imagination of a man is healthy. But there is a space of life between in which the soul is in a ferment, the character undecided, the way of life uncertain, the ambition thick-sighted. Thence proceeds mawkishness. . . .' *Foglie d'Alloro*, as the book was called, rather than being a finished work is only a sign of the first sparks of poetry in Dun Karm, which in time were destined to flare up and set afire the Żebbuġ poet's sensitive heart with an undying flame. Of the thirty-seven poems in this collection, only a few do not treat their subject in the conventional fashion. In them one can feel the rhythm of the Italian poet Monti whom Dun Karm, under the influence of his teacher Giovanni Eliseo del Ricco, had learned to love and revere. Nevertheless, anyone reading *Foglie d'Alloro* cannot but admire the perfect command of Italian which Dun Karm possessed so early in life, and which later he was to adorn with really beautiful poems that earned for him the name of the Maltese Zanella.

As we have said, during this period the Italian poet Dun Karm was under the influence of Vincenzo Monti (1754–1818), the author of *Bassvilliana* and other poems distinguished by the truly musical quality of their lines. But let us leave the young Dun Karm of long ago himself to express, in this sonnet from *Foglie d'Alloro*, his great esteem for this Italian poet, who with Giacomo Zanella proved later in his life to

be one of the sources from which he drew the living
waters of Maltese poetry.

A Vincenzo Monti

Quando al chiarore di notturno lume,
Mentre grato ai mortali il sonno scende,
Dispiego, O Monti, il ricco tuo volume,
E nel tuo gran pensier l'anima intende,

Io ti vedo spiegar l'agili piume
Alle regioni e il fulmine s'accende,
E teco mi trascendi ed il costume
Obblio del mondo e solo il ciel mi splende.

Quindi mi balza il cor, quindi dal seno
Una voce mi fugge: O dell' Ausonio
Apollineo ciel astro sereno,

Te dal Baltico mar fino all' Jonio
Imiti Europa e le castalie Dive,
Rasciutto il pianto, torneran giulive.

Also from *Foglie d'Alloro*, we take the sonnet to his
father which appears to be the only one dedicated to
him; for in his Maltese poems Dun Karm hardly ever
mentions his father, save in passing in the poem
Żjara lil Ġesù. Here then is the sonnet on his father.

A Mio Padre Morto

Tu sparisti, o gentil, e sol nel cuore
Mi lasciasti tua immagine scolpita:
Or ti chiamo sovente e al mio dolore
Non risponde che l'Eco impietosita.

Ahimè! perchè la gioia dell' amore
Si riconosce più quando sparita?
Tu più bello mi sembri or che d' orrore
Le fibre mi gelò la tua partita.

Ed, oh, potesser nella fredda fossa
Sotto il calor di ripetuti baci
Redivive esultar le tue aride ossa;

Che io non saprei da quell' urna staccarmi
E co' miei labbri, che non son mendaci,
Logororei piangendo i duri marmi.

It is a fine sonnet, which time swept into oblivion, leaving the love of his mother to burn alone in the heart of the ageing poet.

After *Foglie d'Alloro* he wrote other poems in Italian, and as it is time that ripens the mind it can be said that his best literary work was produced after this first collection. In 1932 Oreste Ferdinando Tencajoli published an anthology of the best Maltese poets writing in Italian. Apart from the propaganda intentions of a book written when the power of Fascist Italy was at its height, and therefore Malta was being regarded as an Italian *irredenta*, this work furnishes us with an excellent bird's-eye view of an important field of Maltese culture at a time when Italian was still at the peak of its influence in Malta. In this anthology we find some very lovely poems by Dun Karm as well. Among these we would mention the poem *Viticoltura*, of which the Maltese poem *Lid-Dielja* appears to be in some parts a translation, in others a free version. The

following three stanzas seem to be the original of the
extract from the Maltese poem cited after them.

> Deh non gitti per noi da sudice
> vecchie tartane e il greco e il siculo
> di floride vigne gli spurghi
> e di nostra bontade non rida,
>
> per dio, più mai. Sogghigna il bretone
> rude insultando: non vedi? fertile
> addita vicino, lontano,
> dei colli il fianco e il piano brullo.
>
> Cogli a vol l'arte: su pali aerei
> con flessuosa lussuria inutile,
> non salga ma prona serpeggi
> di poco tralcio ricca la vite.

From *Lid-Dielja*:

> Halli iżjed ma narawx fuq xatt gżiritna
> Minn dgħajes qodma u maħmuġin jitferragħ
> Taparsi nbid li minnu l-ebda qatra
> Ma taf id-dielja;
>
> Halli ma nisimgħux lil min jagħdirna,
> U jidħak bina minnufih: mhix tjieba
> It-tjieba żejda; bluha kbira tixtri
> Il-mewt bi flusek.
>
> O Malta tiegħi, ma rajthiex id-daħka,
> Ma smajthiex tfaqqa' fuq xuftejn barrani?
> Urih imlibbsa kullimkien bid-dwieli
> Għoljiet xemxija.

Tħarisx lejn dari; la tistmellx is-sengħa
Ġdida li tgħarrfek kif ittuq id-dielja:
Iżbor u qaċċat: tħallihiex tisserdak . . .

And the closing lines of *Viticoltura*:

non te d'inconsci fantasmi torbidi
malferma ebbrezza nel fango accerchia:
ne' tomba si chiuda precoce
sul tuo figlio per morir sol nato.

And from *Lid-Dielja*:

Hekk huwa ma jiskirx, ma jħassarx demmu,
Moħħu jkun f'sikktu, qalbu tkun qawwija,
U fuq uliedu ma jingħalaq kmieni
Għatu ta' qabar.

The Italian verses which we have quoted should
suffice to testify to the facility with which our poet
could employ the Italian language, and how well he
merited the name of the Maltese Zanella. As further
witness to this facility I would like to add the first
five of the forty-one stanzas of his poem *A Cristo*
(1921).

Solo e sublime stai fra cielo e terra
securo il piede su granito eterno,
— uomo e divino, sacerdote e rege —
candido Cristo.

Vanno le aquile intorno al tuo bel capo
con forte volo: posa al tuo calcagno
maestoso leon; tu mansüeto
guardi e sorridi:

84

Sorridi e guardi e vedi col possente
occhio di sole comparir da lunge,
passarti innanzi e via fuggir nel buio
uomini e tempi.

Tal un antico bruno scoglio, nido
di fuggenti gabbiani, uso a le bianche
ire del mar, vede inoffeso intorno
scorrer i flutti,

E mentre basso con sinistri lampi
gli rugghia il cielo e si lamenta il vento,
oltre le nubi, su la cima, chiaro
gli splende il sole.

Concerning his Italian poetry O. F. Teneajoli
wrote as follows in his above mentioned anthology:

La poesia di Mons. Psaila è essenzialmente educativa;
virgiliano come lo Zanella, egli ama le armonie della
natura. La sua vena ha un po' del settecento veneziano
calmo e dorato, la sua melodia dolce e riposante in-
spirata tuttavia a sentimenti classici è ricca di facoltà
simpatiche come quella del poeta vicentino. Natura
raccolta e grave, senza esser un solitario, ingegno acuto
nelle sue liriche sobrie e tornite si sente la forza della
tradizione e l'energia spontanea e vigile della stirpe.
Questo maestro di lingua e di gusto estetico, non si è
creato come tanti poeti fanno, un mondo a parte e
fantastico; è rimasto nella realtà. In lui equilibrio ed
armonia si fondono in una magnifica sinfonia di grazia
serena, di luce e di colori dalle smaglianti tonalità. Tutti
questi pregi conferiscono alle sue poesie un valore di
eccezione, sia per la purezza della lingua che per la forma
artistica. Esse sono destinate a segnare nella storia
letteraria di Malta una bella pagina.

No one writing in a foreign language could expect higher praise. Being a real master of Italian, he could express himself in that language as well as any native; and his was not a laboured Italian, but an Italian which many Italians praised and admired.

However, this dexterity of our poet in the Italian language would never have sufficed by itself to carry his poetry to every Maltese, rich or poor, town-dweller or countryman, educated or unlettered. However beautiful they were, these Italian verses resembled a closed garden where the multitudes were not permitted to enter. So for these people he was not a poet; for these countrymen of his, starved of good reading, his talents as a writer were worthless—they could not make any use of them, just as they could make no use of the great foreign poets and prose-writers whom they were unable to understand in the original. In a way, Dun Karm was selling his Muse to foreigners. As soon as Dun Karm became aware of this he abandoned Italian for Maltese. This is how he speaks of his change in his fine sonnet *Lill-Muża*. In his old age the poet sees with pleasure the great number of young people who, attracted by his poetry, are dedicating themselves to the Maltese Muse, and recalling the time when he wrote only in Italian, he contentedly tells the Maltese Muse:

> Nor shall I grieve if from the pupils of my eyes
> the light of the last sun flees, and with you
> I make encounter no more: here died, in my hands,
> he who, alas, once bartered you to the stranger.

Dun Karm's conversion to Maltese was the most significant event in the history of our language, and

for this we owe our gratitude to Ġ. Muscat-Azzopardi;
for it was he who in 1921 first persuaded him to
write a poem in Maltese for *Il-Habib*. More than any
other poet before him, Dun Karm raised the Maltese
tongue from the dust in which it had been trampled
for so long, and elevated it on a high pedestal from
which, for many years, its relentless enemies wished to
depose it, with the unexpected result of firmly riveting
it upon the rock as a national monument for ever. The
high ideals which guided the heart and mind of
Dun Karm in this struggle are commemorated in his
poem *Għaliex?* Until only a few years ago some
blind people, just as today there are still some who
lose their heads after foreigners, combated Maltese
by maintaining that its teaching was detrimental to the
learning of other languages. To these Dun Karm, the
master not only of Maltese but also of Italian, replies
in this poem. Why should you cast away the language
of your own native land? Study foreign languages if
these are useful to you, 'but place not outside that
which belongs inside'. The best Maltese writers show
clearly how right Dun Karm was when he argued that
in itself, the study of Maltese was not detrimental to
other languages; for like him, some Maltese are
excellent linguists.

Let us now pass to consider Dun Karm as a Maltese
poet. The first thing to note is his easy mastery over
the Maltese vocabulary: his skill in choosing the right
word to convey the power or sweetness of his ideas,
and to place it in the right sequence so as to produce
a wave of harmony and a fullness of rhythm pleasing
to the ear. For one who is not a poet, and whose ear

does not respond to the beautiful currents of rhythm, every word is as good as any other. But for the poet, every word corresponds with a definite musical note. For him every word is built up of consonantal and vocalic elements which together produce various musical phrases according to the interweaving of these two elements, precisely as in music. Thus the words *dielja*, *ġenna*, *art* are in themselves sweeter than such harsher words as *għaxja*, *ċħatar*, *ħommos*. The liquid sounds *l*, *m*, *n*, *r*, *v*, are in themselves much sweeter than *q*, *għ*, *ż*, *ġ*. But the less sweet sounds are very often charged with greater power and can create a music even more expressive in its harshness, like German music as compared with Italian. Now the ability of the poet to produce a pleasing effect on the heart and mind of the reader naturally depends on his mastery to distribute and harmonize the sounds which together build up the word, the poet's instrument. Dun Karm shows us this mastery in the art of producing sweetness or power, among other places in his poem *Warda li Tgħid Ġrajjietha* and in his sonnet *Nhar San Ġwann*. In the first we are fascinated by the sheer beauty of words radiant as the hills basking in the morning sun, lit up by that fresh imagination which gives them a variegated colouring of graceful ideas and an alternation of sweet rhythms. Observe the imaginative grace and precision of words in the verses that follow, which are most apt to bring to one's mind and heart the sad strains of the violin, sorrowful as a rose trodden underfoot.

> Id-daqq tbiddel: il-mewġa ferrieħa
> Kisret f' oħra ta' ħasret il-qalb:

Il-vjolini titniehed, titbekka,
Kollox ilħna ta' ħniena, ta' talb.

Bdiet iż-żifna meqjusa max-xejra
Tal-vjolini li tofrogħ u tfur,
U l-iżwieġ fuq il-qiegħa bħal ħġieġa,
Bdiet titbandal, tixxengel u ddur.

The music changed: the joyous wave
Broke into another saddening the heart:
The violins were sighing, weeping
With voices of yearning, of supplication.

The dance began, measured to the rhythm
Of the violins ebbing and flowing,
And the couples on the glassy dance-floor
Began to rock, to sway, to revolve.

Or consider the beauty of this picturesque description of a girl who has just plucked a tearful rose from
its mother's bosom to adorn herself.

Snows that glitter on a wintry Etna
Were the garments that veiled her closely,
A patch of sky the mantle that hid her
From the inquisitive eyes of men.

With these verses let us compare the following
taken from the sonnet *Nhar San Ġwann* which, as
befits the subject, are more solemn.

Long centuries have passed, and your voice remains
Beautiful and strong on the day of the solemn feast,
The voice of the great Baptist echoing in the early dawn
Over this city, builded never to fall.

Whoever reads Dun Karm's poetry cannot but picture the author steeped in admiration of the very speech that lends him such power over thought itself. For him the word is a mystery, a mighty matter: a creature of God: a garment of thought.

O Word! O Word! What art thou?
Whence camest thou? When wert thou born?
Camest thou from God in a lightning flash,
Or hast thou evolved with time?

However thou camest, thou art the loveliest, greatest
Of all the many wonders of earth;
Whenever my mind is fixed on thee
I glimpse a light like the light of heaven.

Besides showing a complete mastery of rhythm, Dun Karm has at his command an equal variety of metres which he employed as if to teach those who did not want to learn, that the Maltese tongue can do anything in the hands of a skilful master. We witness his skill mostly in his great power of building the sonnet, that flows like a compact, solid musical wave from the arresting opening to the verses of the close which fall as solemn as the tolling of the great bell on St. John's Day.

Of all the different forms of prosody the sonnet is the most difficult, because within its short compass it must obey more or less fixed rules of harmony and construction. The sonnet has its own regulations, its own code of laws; if these are broken, it will not be possible to produce a good sonnet according to the technique laid down by the greatest foreign writers. Young poets who are still in training, so to speak, are very often deceived when they think that they can write sonnets from the very beginning, just as if, because they only contain fourteen verses, they are not as difficult to compose as longer forms of poetry.

As regards technique, the Maltese sonnet is of two kinds: the Shakespearian with the formula *abab cdcd efef gg* which is not found in Dun Karm, and the Petrarchian divided into two quatrains and two tercets rhyming *abab abab cdc ede*, or with the tercets *cde cde*, or even *abba abba cdc ede*. These are the patterns of Dun Karm's sonnets. The first two sections are called quatrains, the last two tercets. The union between both sections, or rather the link between the last lines of the quatrains and the first of the tercets, is not left to chance but is guided by more or less fixed rules.

A rule to keep in mind when reading or criticizing a sonnet is that, while the sonnet taken as a whole is a poetic unity, a single piece of music, a tune that is formed out of diverse notes, there must be a pause or a break between the first eight verses and the last six. That is to say, in reading the sonnet we feel that the first eight lines are detached from the last six. Thus the two sections form two distinct waves of a single piece of music, which then reunite in the total effect when the whole sonnet has been read through. In a good sonnet the two waves are felt to blend into one, just as two waves of the sea unite when they come together. So it will be as if we have actually two separate poems which come together to form a single one. However, although the sestine almost forms a separate poem with its own structure, its sense is dependent on that of the octave. Hence the sestine must be not less beautiful or powerful than the octave, otherwise the final effect on the mind and ear of the reader will be unpleasing. Moreover, in the sonnet there must be no more than this one pause between sestine and octave, apart from the caesuras which being only rhythmical pauses which do not affect the sense are therefore legitimate, and indeed beautify and adorn the music of the sonnet. As to the subject, this should be either emotional or reflective, or both combined as in many of the best sonnets. From this it follows that the sonnet is not manageable in the hands of one who is not emotional or reflective or both simultaneously.

As a sonnet writer Dun Karm has never been surpassed by any other Maltese author, and does not compare unfavourably with the great sonnet writers of foreign countries. Real jewels as regards both thought and technique are sonnets like *Wied Qirda*, *Nhar San Ġwann*, *Bjuda*, *Il-Knisja*, *Mater Purissima*, and others. Their mood is reflective rather than emotional, but both emotion and reflection very often merge in Dun Karm, like rays of the sun focused by a lens on a single point. We shall cite only two examples. The first is the sonnet *Lil Ġannina Pisani*. Because the mood of Dun Karm's Muse is less emotional than reflective his Maltese expresses itself with dignity and is impressive, because it is full of that solemnity of thought and feeling of a poet meditating and singing in the presence of the august mysteries of life, the events of the times, the history of his own people and their language, and of the Church. A palpable difference in style can be observed between two poets of whom one is more emotional and the other more reflective. Both the wave of thought and the garment in which that thought is clothed are different. This difference may be recognized by comparing the reflective sonnets of Milton with those of Keats, the sonnets of Dun Karm with those of Ġorġ Pisani. There is sweetness of emotion in the one, but solemnity in the other—that solemnity of the great bell among the lesser bells in our steeples, scattering abroad an air of solemnity and of great moment.

The same reflective element clothes the thought of Dun Karm in his religious poetry in a different metre, such as *Żjara lil Ġesù*. The two opening lines are the key to the disposition of the poet's mind and heart. There is no bubbling over or upsurge of emotion, that uncontrolled bubbling of water as it leaps over rocks, which kindles the enthusiasm of the young more especially; but they are full of the deep meditations of a poet who keeps himself well under control and bridles the agitation of his heart with the reins of the mind—controlled emotion.

Never shall I forget the sweetness I felt within me that time, O Jesus.

It is the beginning of recollection and the beginning of reflection. This is the poetry of the *Imitatio Christi* of Thomas à Kempis, the poetry of certain pages of the *Confessions* of St. Augustine, the poetry of a priest who has given his heart to Christ—a priest who thinks and feels, but is measured in both his speech and his thought—a self-controlled poet, continually watching for the snares of Circe's song, so dangerous to even

93

him as a poet, and because the beauty of the world is to be feared, and fear brings discipline; and from the discipline of the heart and mind alone is born the reflective mood of the priest-poet. The reflective element is a good recipient of the descriptive element. Between the two exists the same relation as between the colour of a thing and the thing itself. Man first looks at life around him and sees it in its own colours, until finally these hues colour his own thoughts. Let us read this description from *Vjatku.*

> Darkness profound; a cold wind whistles
> Through the window cracks, and on the closed panes
> The drizzling rain incessantly patters,
> > And from the spouts
>
> Water spills down the streets. On the glaze
> Of the drenched ground here and there shivers
> The red glow of the lamps, as if they were
> > Beckoning to sleep.

This is a painter who, on the canvas of his mind, paints a night scene: darkness, cold, rain, ground glistening, reflection of the lamps. But this scene is only the background for the Viaticum, which remains the highest thought of the poet in this composition. All these details, however, the whole of the descriptive element, rain and darkness, glossy ground and lamp reflections, colour the poet's thought. The reflective poet makes extensive use of the descriptive element in his poetry, because the object of reflection is either a thing with its own colours or an abstract event which wears the colours given it by people who have been struck by it.

We are stressing this point especially on account of those people who think that only that is poetry which bubbles forth hastily, wearing the loud colours of the Muse of youth.

Among the religious poems of Dun Karm are *Alla Mhux Hekk*, *Lil Kristu Sultan*, *Il-Mewt ta' S. Wistin*, and another, *Waħda Biss*, which is a reply to an even better known poem by R. Briffa, *Wieħed Biss*. This poem conveys a very lofty idea. It shows us God as an artist who creates not one masterpiece only which is defaced by time, but 'makes a hundred every day and a hundred expunges'. Moreover we find in this poem the same jewel-like diction which we see in *Warda li Tgħid Ġrajjietha*. Here is a description of a sunset.

> There was in the summer sky
> filling the air a fine spray
> of liquid gold and powdered topaz
>
> and houses and fields and trees
> all burning beneath the crimson kiss
> of the great, compassionate sun.

In the poem *Il-Mewt ta' Santu Wistin*, as in others of his poems, besides the literary beauty and the technical mastery, we hear also that surge of full, measured rhythm which makes Dun Karm's poetry like a classical symphony. And like Milton, so famous for his skill in producing sweetness out of proper names by weaving them with other words into the metre of the verse, our poet makes use of foreign names in a most harmonious fashion. Here are the opening lines of this poem.

The flood is spreading over Mauritania
Of the Vandals, the Alans under Gaiseric,
Trampling, shattering, destroying all things
    Lying in its wake.

O Bonifacius, late you repented. Timely
And prudent was the wise Augustine's
Peace-loving counsel; but within your heart
    Jealousy triumphed.

We observe the same mastery in the sonnet *Wied
Qirda.*

As I descend here, at the time when crimson
The sun is hidden behind il-Fuqqanija . . .
And I feel Death passing over Wied Qirda.

Each place-name has the sound of a musical note.

In Dun Karm's religious poetry we feel the comfort
of that faith which accepts everything from the hand
of God, the faith of a poet filled with the love of
Christ and of the Catholic Church, to which he also
dedicated one of his most powerful sonnets, of the
Blessed Sacrament, of the Madonna. But while Dun
Karm shows more affection in his Maltese poetry for
his mother than for his father, in his religious verse
he is more struck by the love and majesty of Christ
the King, Christ hidden in the Holy Eucharist, than
by the Blessed Virgin. The poet *par excellence* of the
Madonna in Maltese literature remains Cuschieri with
his fiery verses full of love which come so natural to
a Carmelite. Christ the King, Christ the Redeemer of
the world, and St. Paul the deliverer of Malta—these
are the themes that recur most often in Dun Karm's

poetry. Of the eleven poems dedicated to or inspired by the Madonna and collected in the second volume of his works, *X'Emmen il-Poeta*, only one soars to heaven and distinguishes itself for its beauty from every other poem. This is the sonnet *Mater Purissima*, a jewel of our literature.

None of the remaining ten reaches the height of the poems about God or St. Paul, of *A Cristo* or *Lil-Monument*. I must repeat, however, that *Mater Purissima* is a jewel of literature which should be learned by heart if only for the music of its verses, the lofty controlled thought, and the fragrance of sublime beauty. The Blessed Virgin has never heard any pane-gyric from the pulpits of our churches that was more lofty: it deserves to take company with *Ave Maria* of Gounod and of Schubert. It is only in this sonnet that Dun Karm has attained and perhaps even surpassed the sublimity of Cuschieri. The others show devotion, but less power than the Carmelite's poems.

If, however, no one has surpassed Cuschieri as the poet of the Madonna, no other poet has as yet excelled Dun Karm as the poet of Christ. The poem *Il-Monument-Tifkira tal-Kungress Ewkaristiku tal-1913* stands alone as one of the greatest Maltese poems on the subject, as do also the verses on the Apostle of Tarsus, whom he commemorates in some of the finest sonnets and poems in our literature.

In the third section of a Dun Karm anthology we see him as a lay poet; lay, that is, only because the subjects of these poems are not sacred. These poems also display the poet's skill in another aspect of the spirit—the spirit in contact with the world. A priest at the altar, he was every day very close to the mysteries of the Eucharist and of religion and sang of them; but being a man like you and me, he also sang of the mysteries of life—love, the family, hatred, envy, and, among other themes, Malta, 'this sweet motherland whose name we bear'.

In this section we find a multitude of really beautiful poems to choose from, many of them already known from other anthologies: *Ġunju*, *Lil-Dielja*, *Dell u Dija*, *Zagħzugħ ta' Dejjem*, and the greatest of them all, *Non Omnis Moriar*, that splendid poem in which Dun Karm engraves himself his own epitaph on the tomb of death vanquished, because his spirit lives on for all that his body dies. There is also the poem *Lil Malta* with the terrible verses:

You were the rose of the world, and became a dunghill
On which all kinds of filth are being thrown;
You receive it and you rejoice, O foolish woman,
    And the world laughs at you!

Malta! If not yet has been written in heaven
Against you the sentence passed on Babylon,
Turn, turn back in your track: He who shall heal you
    Awaits you in Sion.

This is the voice of the poet-prophet who sometimes chides; and prophecy is one of the highest gifts of poetic inspiration. There are moments when poet and prophet speak with one tongue, the tongue of prophecy. This reproach of the poet recalls in its solemn dignity a similar reproach uttered by

Dante against the Florentines of his time, soulless robbers.

Godi, Fiorenza, poi che sei si grande
Che per mare e per terra batti l'ali,
E per l'inferno il tuo nome si spande.

(Inf. c. xxvi, 1–3.)

Whoever reproaches his own native land in such harsh words does so because he loves no less ardently the beloved country in which he was born and lived his life, the country which for Dun Karm is the jewel in St. Paul's crown, one of the most ancient and most precious links in the chain of Catholicism in Europe. That same love which compels him to rage against those who are ruining his homeland also constrains him to reproach, as a Pauline Maltese, a dignitary of that same Church of which he is minister when this person, Monsignor Palunko Bishop of Spalato, in 1910, in the words of our poet 'was pleased to revive the ancient controversy whether St. Paul actually came to Malta or went to another island called Meleda; and made no little fuss about St. Paul never having come to Malta at all'.

Dun Karm's patriotism is of the kind which, without blowing its own trumpet or parading itself, disdainful and vainglorious with foreigners, plants in the poet's heart a torch which constantly shines with the purest love and deepest reverence for the land which gave us birth. History will always remind us that it was Dun Karm, the second President of the Society of Maltese Writers after Ġuże' Muscat-Azzopardi, who gave the Maltese people their national anthem which is now rightly played at all public functions, in schools, and in other gatherings. From the Maltese movement emerged that true patriotism which does not strike its roots outside our own little plot, but in real Maltese soil. What benefit could the Maltese derive from those patriotic poems of other writers of ours who composed praises to Malta in a language which the majority of Maltese do not understand, and those few who do feel as foreign as any language which is not learned in the home but at school? For this reason Dun Karm's national anthem filled a wide gap in our national life. With his tongue he brought unity where formerly there was separation. The poet says to Malta in his *Għanja tar-Rebħa*:

But in your own tongue I shall sing you that song
Which deep in my heart I have shaped for you
And write it with the blood my mother gave me,
Desirous, O Malta, to give you your due honour;

For Maltese was the blood that dripped red hot
On your battlements, the richest pledge of fame!
Maltese the heart that in a sea of sorrows
Held firm till the glorious day of victory dawned.

And in his Maltese national anthem he prays thus to God:

Keep watch, O Lord, as Thou hast watched for ever
O'er this sweet motherland whose name we bear,
Arrayed by Thee in radiance most fair:
Grant to her rulers wisdom, just endeavour
To master-man, to worker health's increase,
Give Malta truest unity and peace.

The poet also composed two fine sonnets which, beside their pure artistic beauty, also serve to generate sentiments of true loyalty and love towards Malta. These are the powerful sonnet *Lil Malta* in which he explains why the love of the islanders should be for Malta rather than any other country, whether it be Italy or Britain; and its companion sonnet *Il-Bandiera Maltija*. As our flag has only two colours, we should add to it neither Italy's green nor Britain's blue.

> So, only white and red; all foreign colours
> That are mingled with your colours, be it blue
> Or be it green, will only deface your name.

> Not only your name deface, but also your body,
> That beautiful body will not remain itself:
> And then . . . in vain will you bewail the past.

We see this same love for Malta, the love of a son for his mother, a love full of sadness, in another sonnet *Lil Malta — Fuq il-Fruntiera — wara elfejn attakk mill-ajru*. It is addressed to Malta as reduced to ruins by the enemy onslaughts of the Fascists and Nazis. With patriotism of such a sweet and noble nature, a patriotism devoid of trumpet-blowing and xenophobia, our young people will grow up to have a greater respect for their native land, and will find it less easy to forget her and disown her when they go abroad and feel that their own country has nothing beautiful to offer of which they can be proud. *Dun Mikiel Xerri* and *Vassalli* reflect the true patriotism in Dun Karm's heart.

Another beautiful love similar to that for Malta is our poet's love of his mother, whom he loved with his whole heart and soul. We saw above from the Italian poem in *Foglie d'Alloro* that he loved his father greatly too, but it was the image of his mother that remained most deeply impressed on his heart and mind with the passage of time. In his longest poem, *Il-Jien u Lil Hinn Minnu*, he says that whenever to his anguish he felt his faith weakening, it was the memory of his mother, a good woman, that brought him back to the light of faith. And it was also the remembrance of his mother that rekindled hope in him when the sorrows of life clung to his heart like briars. We find his mother mentioned in many of his poems.

Having tried to penetrate into the heart and mind of the poet, we must now say something of the technique of his verses. Dun Karm is a classical writer not only in his thought and the way he expresses it, but also in his choice of metrical forms. For this reason it is vain to search for the least echo of the modernest wave that has engulfed the art of the twentieth century. And fortunately so, for the destiny of the art of this troubled century is very uncertain; and though friends of the modern movement are not lacking who call to mind other movements which are now antiquated but were considered revolutionary in their day, and were thought by many people not to be able to hold out against time whereas they did survive, there is good reason to suspect that in our days the modernist movement has gone far beyond the bounds and is remote from the spirit, the greatness and the beauty of thought and word. Dun Karm's poetry, like the poetry of every leader of a movement, has enriched our literature with phrases, words, and poetic expressions, as well as with a variety of metrical forms. Unhappily Dun Karm's fame has sometimes provoked a suspicion among some foreigners, who love to meddle in our affairs and never desired that Maltese should come into its own, fearing that with the revival of the language the Maltese nation would also be reborn, thus weakening the pretensions of other nations on Malta and the Maltese, especially those of our neighbour Italy.

Thus some critics thought that in the title Zanella of Malta they could recognize a slavish copying by Dun Karm of the Italian poet. One of the loveliest and best known of Dun Karm's poems is *Il-Musbieħ tal-Mużew*. About this pearl of Maltese literature Ettore Rossi, who was more of a historian than a literary critic, wrote: 'Il ritmo di questa poesia nel testo maltese ricorda l'ode *Sopra una Conchiglia Fossile* dello Zanella ed anche l'intonazione e il pensiero sono identici.'

One can easily understand the motives that prompted Ettore Rossi to make the second part of this remark, based on a pure misunderstanding, if we recall that he wrote these words in a book entitled *Lingua Italiana, Dialetto Maltese e Politica Brittanica a Malta* (Livorno, R. Giusti, ed., 1929, pp. 55–56). It cannot be denied that the metres are similar; but so are the metres of certain poets like Dante, Petrarch, Milton, and others who composed sonnets, for the simple reason that the sonnet has a fixed form. This does not mean however that one writer stands on another's shoulders because the other used the sonnet form before him. Metre is the measure of verse along with its other elements, which are rhythm and, sometimes, rhyme. If a poet writes in blank verse this does not mean that he is dependent on those who did so before him. There may be a similarity of the forms chosen, but so long as there is no plagiarism or borrowing or taking over of ideas from another poet, the metrical similarity does not diminish in any way the poet's merit. In his poem *Sopra una Conchiglia Fossile* Zanella draws his inspiration from a fossilized shell which he kept on his desk and used as a paper-weight. As the poet was interested in the discoveries of science, he imagined that he beheld in that fossil the geological periods of the world when the earth was passing through so many changes, before it cooled to the temperature which would allow man to inhabit it. In this the Vicentine poet foresees the glorious time when man will have made such intellectual progress that the powers of the soul will overcome the lower instincts, and so a much higher civilization than the contemporary one will be established in the world.

On the other hand Dun Karm derives the theme of his poem from an old oil lamp preserved in the Museum for its historical value. This lamp appears to be so old because of the fish engraved on it; and as in the second century a fish was used by Christians as a symbol for Christ, the poet sees in the lamp a reminder of the times when the first Christians used to go into the catacombs to celebrate their mysteries. These times are so remote that we now know virtually nothing of conditions then, not even what language the Maltese spoke. But one thing has never changed, the Church of the Crucified. We can well see that both poems draw their argument from antiquity: Zanella from prehistory, Dun Karm from ancient history. Thus both had to use short verses to run through the centuries from the beginning to the present day. Dun Karm chose a six-syllable verse with stanzas of four lines rhymed in the second and the fourth, while Zanella uses seven-verse stanzas with lines of six syllables rhyming *ababcdd*. As I wrote in the note on this poem in the third volume of *Ward ta' Qari Malti* (1940, p. 242): 'While we agree that the rhythm of these two poems is similar on account of the similarity of the metre used in both, we do not agree that there is similarity of thought, as is evident if one studies and compares the two poems. To run through two thousand years in such a short poem, Dun Karm had to employ short verses with a light rhythm.'

Therefore the similarity between Zanella and Dun Karm is like the similarity between two brothers, and not the similarity of dependence. To explain our meaning further: both poets were priests, and though Giosue Carducci once said that if it were left to him he would never permit priests to write poetry, both did in fact write so well that they brought honour to their native Muse; Zanella even merited the praise of the anti-clerical Carducci. As priests both sucked the milk of the same mother, the Catholic Church; both had to keep a watch on themselves in their writing, a discipline which could not allow them to take liberties with the Muse in affairs of this world, especially as regards the love of women. For this reason the love of woman is in both sublimated into a higher love, that of their religion and of their native land. Indeed, both Dun Karm and Zanella are patriots, and both directed their manly love towards their mothers. When Zanella's mother was dying, he addressed her thus in his poem *A Mia Madre*.

> Rimani, o pia, la vita
> Quali dolcezze a te serbi ignoro;
> Ma di tua santa aita
> Ancor uopo ha quest' alma; ancor t'imploro
> A' virili anni miei fido riparo,
> Come già fosti al fanciulletto ignaro.
>
> Madre! Il tuo caro viso,
> I santi detti tuoi che a me bambino
> Su i tuoi ginocchi assiso,
> Furon maestri, ancor contento inchino,
> Semplici detti; ma l'ingegno umano
> Forse con frutto scandagliò l'arcano?

These sentiments are similar to those in *Jien u Lil Hinn Minnu*, Dun Karm's longest philosophical poem, and to phrases in other poems where this humble poet recalls his mother's love. As priests, both sang to their native land. Among other poems, Zanella wrote in his *Ad un Amico* that he regretted the wrongs which Italy had suffered, but he still had a firm hope that Italy *non muore*; and Dun Karm in his *Għanja tar-Rebħa*, *Lil Malta* and elsewhere wrote similarly. For both, the Catholic religion is the torch that sheds the strongest light on the darkness of existence, and both accept its teaching without doubt, without questioning. For both, as Dante says:

> Fede è sostanza di cose sperate
> Ed argomento delle non parventi.

For both, creation is a song of love. For Zanella, as he himself says in his *Voci Secrete*, creation is an *immenso tempio d'amore*, a thought which Dun Karm repeats in his poem *Il-Għanja ta' l-Imħabba*. Both of them recognized the link between science and religion which, in Zanella's times, when Darwinism was still a new doctrine, appeared to threaten the life of the Church's dogma. Both appear to have had their moments of doubt during the convulsions of life, black moments when the spirit, hurt and confused, filled the heart of the priest-poet with melancholy. In Dun Karm, the conflict between Reason and Faith appears in the battle between the heart and the mind, as depicted in his *Jien u Lil Hinn Minnu*. With the death of Ġannina Pisani, who was for him like a daughter, still fresh in his memory he often asked himself:

Whence the beginning? Where the end? What signify
The Good and Evil in the weaving of life
Hurried in such short time? Is it not a dream,
The compassionate goodness that my mother taught
    me
In the school of her lap?

Zanella too in his poem *Dopo una lettura dell'Imitazione di Cristo* makes us think that he was troubled and confused by certain doubts, which he most likely did not always overcome, when science was fiercely attacking the doctrines of the Church. But in Zanella's heart, as in Dun Karm's, after darkness the light of faith shines forth, as we can see in the following verses taken from the same poem.

Nel mio mortal sbigottimento a gli anni
Di più candida fè volsi un sospiro.

And in his other fine poem *La religione materna* he likens himself to a pilgrim who, because he allowed his eyes to be attracted by other lights, did not heed the lamp his mother gave him to see his way, until darkness returned and once more the light of that lamp showed him the right road, the road pointed out by the common mother of both poets, the Catholic Church.

A tremolar distinta,
Torna la fiamma ch'ei credeva estinta

Such a similarity of sentiments could not be lacking in the two poets who drank of the same source, and made communion with the same Body and Blood of the same Redeemer on the altar of one Church.

We can see that Dun Karm loved Zanella also from a translation he made of one of the Vicentine's loveliest poems, *Egoismo e Carità* which, according to Carducci, is 'degna d'Orazio e dei lirici greci dell' Antologia'. To demonstrate the skill of our poet as a translator we shall cite the last two stanzas, first in Italian and then in Maltese. The poet Zanella sings to the vine which gives wine to the old man in the cold of winter.

Tu piangi derelitta a capo chino,
Sulla ventosa balza. In chiuso loco
Gaio frattanto il vecchierel vicino
Si asside al foco.

Tien colmo un nappo; il tuo licor gli cade
Nell'ondeggiar del cubito sul mento;
Poscia floridi paschi ed auree biade
   Sogna contento.

In Maltese:

B'rasek lejn l-art milwija int titbekka
Fuq il-quċċata kollha rjieħ. Ġo daru
Nilmaħ fil-waqt ix-xwejjaħ ġar minn tiegħek
   Ma' ġenb il-maġmar,

B'tazza f'idu mimlija; fuq ilħitu,
Fir-rogħda ta' dirgħajh, l-inbid ixerred:
Imbagħ'd mergħa sabiħa u sbul imdieheb
   Joħlom fi friexu.

Besides this poem, our poet translated into Maltese
four verses of Goethe (*Ħlewwiet Moħbija*), *San Pawl*
from Cardinal John Henry Newman, G. Pascoli's
La Quercia Caduta, Thomas Hardy's *The Oxen*, three
proverbial verses from Shakespeare, and best and
loftiest of all, *L-Oqbra*, a version of Ugo Foscolo's *I
Sepolchri*, a poem which fills the gap left by the denial
of faith by means of the love of fame achieved through
poetry, that pagan love which drew from Dun Karm
an answer in *Jien u Lil Hinn Minnu*. He also translated
some verses from less known poets.

In this study we have seen how high Dun Karm has
soared over the mountain-peaks of poetry. Posterity
will certainly value no less than we the heritage of
beauty which Dun Karm has left to these islands, as
long as the Maltese language continues to be read.
And because beauty is always loved, it will not matter
at all if in the heaven of literature other stars and

planets of magnitude appear; Dun Karm's name will never die from among us. He was assuredly right when he applied to himself in one of his finest poems the line of Horace:

NON OMNIS MORIAR.

Ġ. AQUILINA

The Gift of Wisdom

THE desire for wisdom is inborn within us. Man is drawn of his very nature towards the knowledge of truth. Indeed, merely show a child, even if he has not yet reached the age of reason, merely show him something new and you will immediately hear him asking what that thing is, what it is called, who made it, to whom it belongs, what purpose it serves, and other questions which go to reveal the intense desire to learn which dwells in his heart, the desire to know the truth.

Everyone wants to learn, everyone desires wisdom, but not everyone craves after the same kind of wisdom. There are some who shed much sweat, pass entire days and nights alike over their books, ruin their health with overwork and with difficult and perilous journeys, to discover some secret, some mystery of nature, to make some invention which will bring them riches and spread the fame of their name throughout the whole world. In spite of the fact that this knowledge of nature leads of its very self to the knowledge of God, to the recognition of His power, of His goodness, and of the fact that He created nature with all its mysteries, the use which man makes of it can be either good or bad, and more often probably bad rather than good. However, even if he makes good use of it, this wisdom is not the gift of the Holy Spirit.

Others wish for, seek after, and go to great expense (as Pope St. Gregory says), to acquire a certain type of wisdom which it would have been far better for them never to have known: the wisdom of this world. Our Holy Father and Apostle gives it the name it deserves, that of foolishness. This wisdom is even farther from being a gift of the Holy Spirit.

The wisdom which is taught by the Holy Spirit consists of those truths which bring us nearer to God and unite us with Him through grace; that adorn the soul with virtue and holiness, enrich it with merits, and guide it to the end for which it was created, eternal repose and joy in the bosom and in the possession of God. This wisdom, as gift of the Holy Spirit, can be summarized in two kinds of knowledge, the knowledge of ourselves and the knowledge of God. Both are so necessary that without either the one or the other we shall not be able to walk on the way that leads to our true fatherland, where we shall contemplate and enjoy God for ever.

We go towards God, as my Holy Father St. Augustine says, not with the feet but with the feelings, desires, and affections that are pleasing to Him. But how can feelings, desires, and love please God unless we know ourselves? If we do not acknowledge our ignorance, on account of which we pronounce as good that which is bad, or the corruption of the desires of our heart that represent vice as virtue, we cannot even begin to cure our spiritual illness which, unless healed, will ruin us and confirm us in sin. If we do not acknowledge the weakness of our souls, the dangers and enemies in and around us, the excuses brought forward by our self-love to justify us when we are wrong, we can neither guard as we should that precious treasure which is to be found within us, nor seek after and take up the arms that are necessary for victory. What therefore can we expect from such weakness and blindness, but lapses?

Hence St. Bernard is right in saying that the first duty of a Christian is to know himself; for it is through this knowledge that humility is engendered, that humility without which no deed can be pleasing to God: 'Sciat primum seipsum: haec scientia humilitatem generat.'

G. M. CAMILLERI, O.S.A.

Lapsi

A GREAT festival of Holy Church reminds us of when our Lord Jesus, having accomplished the ransoming of man, rose up to heaven after addressing his Apostles. Before all the multitude, the Lord ascended and a cloud received him out of their sight. Two men clothed in white appeared in the midst and were heard to say: 'Ye men of Galilee, why stand ye gazing up into heaven? This same Jesus, which is taken up from you into heaven, shall so come in like manner.'

The word Lapsi, taken from the Greek, for us implies rejoicing. The good people in their faith mention the wonders that took place on that day. The Maltese say that at midnight of that blessed day the sea loses its salt which makes it bitter and unpalatable, and becomes sweet.

To this day they chant in our villages:

> Be sweet, O sea, be sweet
> as you are sweet on the night of Lapsi,
> if you go around the whole world
> you won't find anyone loves you like me.

I remember the time when at the approach of Lapsi, in all the creeks around the island, San Pawl il-Baħar, San Ġiljan, Tas-Sliema, l-Imsida, il-Fossa, the shores of l-Isla, il-Karkara, Wied il-Għajn, Birżebbuġa, wherever 'walnut-shells' were to be found tied up, there you would see its owner unfurling the sails and lifting the anchor to catch the morning breeze that had just begun to be felt, and seeking to set forth into the open to glide on the surface of the water, happy as a bird, with his flag fluttering at the mast-head, the sun hot as fire on his face and the bells ringing out around him from all the churches in the land. Luff now and take the wind and fill the sails: it's daybreak!

The people living by the sea, after church was over, used to scatter in search of some sheltered corner on the rocks where they could be near the sweet coolness of the water, for the heat of the atmosphere now began to be felt in earnest. All along the beaches you could see, behind some great rock at the entrance of a grotto or under some brink of shore, sheets, blankets, flags dangling and hanging down, anything that might cast a bit of shade which at midday might extinguish the heat of the sun. And so all through that festival holiday the people amused themselves and rested from their daily labours.

The women went round with pots and pans and built fireplaces with stones and pebbles from the beach, and lighted fires to cook what they had brought with them in bags, baskets, panniers, bundles. The men with rolled-up sleeves looked to see if they could catch anything from the sea, 'ringing' for octopus, casting a line for young rock-cod, hanging down fishing-cords for sargus or gudgeon, throwing bait for black-tail, while others stooped after limpets, snails, sea-anemones, and if they could lay hands on a grab, after any sea-urchins in the vicinity.

The children happy as birds played with whatever they could find; if it was sand, they puddled in it and threw pebbles to watch them glide over the surface when they struck the sea, crying out at the top of their voices: 'bread and sardines'—'see how mine jumped out'—'mine bounced three times'—'mine always sinks'. And the mothers, shouting and getting into a rage: 'Pawlu, come here. . . . Ninu, just see how drenched you've got! Ġuzeppi, let go of that and come out of that pool; Mari, mind you don't fall into the sea, come back now. . . .' And the children would laugh and have fun, picking up pebbles and sending them spinning, while all the time the women shrieked and got angry.

As noon approached the sun really scorched, and the pangs of hunger began to be felt. Very slowly the children stole towards a slice of bread, the women spread a sheet or some other covering on the ground and prepared the plates for serving the meal, and the smell of boiling and roasting began to waft abroad, and everyone started to creep softly towards the shade and the smell of food and to take up his place to trifle with something. A few words, then everyone stretched forth his hands and brought them up to his mouth. Wine was not lacking, and after hours in the sun and that fragrant food, the drop in the flask went down like honey. The sounds and cries little by little diminished, and the one desire of everybody was to repose awhile in the shade.

Anyone who had a guitar didn't leave it at home; there was always some girl fond of singing, and some lad togged up in his first long trousers encouraged to show off his voice. And the people laughed and were happy, until the time came for everyone to lend a hand to pack up, to wrap up something or other, to fill baskets and hampers and to load the boats once more for the homeward journey.

The people living far from the sea passed the time about their own cottages, in the gardens, in the squares, happy with their children and kinsfolk. The kiddies were soon thinking about swings, for Lapsi without a swing was something unheard of. Vitor would bring a cord from a shed, Mari would get hold of a rope even if she had to unfasten it from a pail, the clothes-line would do just as well. Now they would find the rope to be all frayed, now it was half rotten, now too long, now too short; but cut, tie, patch, and finally it would reach the desired length.

'Where do you say we hang it, love?'

'Is the rope strong, Grezz? Mind no one gets hurt.'

'We'll tie it to those two tree-trunks. They're old carob-trees, so what's there to be afraid of?'

'The big swing between the carob-trees, the little one from the garret window.'

'Call Gori to help you tie it, Lunzjat.'

One girl fetches the ladder, another ties the cord, another stretches out a piece of plank as a seat, this one spreads under an old petticoat folded in four, that one adds a couple of feet of cord so that one can swing from it, and the game begins and goes on and on until it is dark. What fun!

Such swinging! such singing! such joking! Żeża sings at the top of her voice, Vitor is angry because her little sister wants to swing in place of her, Mananni shrieks because they are pushing her up so high.

Pawla wants someone to give her a big shove, Ġulina is convulsed with laughter because she fell on her back when the rope slipped out of the knot.

> Tonight is the night of Lapsi,
> The townspeople draw out the boats;
> A basket of cherries
> On the bridal table. . . .

One song is followed by another, to the handclapping and whistling of the boys and the laughter of the girls.

> My mother made me a swing,
> She made it me on top of the house;
> There wasn't anyone to swing me,
> Gori climbed up on his knees. . . .

And on they go until the sun sinks behind the hills, and the mothers and grannies say that will do.

So the Feast of Lapsi comes and goes like other festivals, and the people with their simple hearts enjoy themselves with amusements proper to the season, and the next morning they get up happy and ready for everyday work as God wants.

TEMI ZAMMIT

The Decision

WHILE this conversation was taking place in the house of Baroness Isabella, when Baroness Klara her friend from Mdina had had her say, and while the slave-girl Halwenija, that young woman whom the prevailing custom of the time had placed on the lowest rung of the social ladder, was doing her best to restore her mistress to consciousness, Alexander had been out of the house for some while, enjoying an hour's respite from the confused conspiracies and political turmoil of those days. Never in a hundred years would he have thought that the Devil would have forced in his head between him and his mother to rob their home of its peace.

He never omitted his daily walk, first of all because the habit of going out into the open and not remaining locked up all day had become for him a spiritual necessity; secondly because silence and the open air strengthened his mind and kept his body fit. On this walk he liked to be alone—he had come across enough people during the day; alone, that is unaccompanied, for he never felt alone in the strict sense of the word. The open air, the earth, the sky and the fields, the variegated hues of leaves and trees, and everything belonging to the created world surrounded him like an overwhelming vision which it is not given to everyone to behold, for not everybody keeps open the eyes of the spirit.

For many people space is just an abstraction, a creation of the mind, something which escapes the touch even more than the wind itself. But for him this word 'the open' was something which could be sensed, something he knew and loved as a saint feels, knows, and loves his very soul! To a saint, that invisible something within us which is the soul is even more substantial than his body. A saint can very well neglect his body; but he will never forget his soul, which is for him the more concrete entity. So it was for Alexander too; the most abstract of thoughts were more real to him than sensible objects: the open air, freedom, friendship, goodness, service, justice, and right clothed themselves within his mind in a garment of flesh and blood, woven into the very fibres of man. Such a youth could only to his own detriment remain on earth, where matter is the monarch and the spirit a slave.

He himself said at times that whenever he was rapt in contemplation of the vastest of creatures, the sky and the sea, he used to forget himself, cast off his body and feel like a pure spirit. Indeed, the farmers around sometimes stopped and stared at him when they beheld him walking with his eyes lifted towards heaven, scrutinizing those blue haunts as if to penetrate the august mystery of that unfathomable vastness. And if anybody happened to stop him, to talk to him when he was thus entranced, he felt a shiver running down his spine, as one who feels he is suddenly dropping from one world into another. For at the sight of all that is grand, he felt as if his spirit struggled within him to free itself of the bonds that tied it to the body, and very often he was heard to remark with a smile: 'If anyone wanted to persuade me that there is no soul I could never believe him, for what is this dynamic force which I feel throbbing within me, restless with longing to tear itself from the body, if it is not the soul? Surely the body, a thing dead and inert, cannot aspire to relinquish itself?'

That morning he was feeling in one of his best moods for contemplation, and for a time he forgot all about the splendour and ugliness of political life, the underground conspiracy in which he had taken part, the spies drowned inside the cistern, and the old hag of Wadi Ghafrid. Everything sank into oblivion, even the widow, and however strange it may seem, he forgot even Pawlina and Ġanni. In that moment he felt himself gripped by a busy host of lofty thoughts darting upon him out of the vastness of the heavens around, met by another stream that radiated from his dynamic spirit. He was experiencing the great union of all creatures with God and felt himself, as man, in the centre of the immensity that enveloped him, to represent a great victory in the plan of the Creator.

Had the circumstances of life permitted Alexander to withdraw into the wilderness, he would assuredly have dedicated himself to the service of Him in Whom and from Whom all things subsist; and in the beauty of the Christian faith of his people he would have burnt his offerings on the altar of the open spaces. In this wilderness he would have become one of those saints who see visions, who weigh whatever is of this world against that which belongs to the next according to its real value, and who fight the good fight against the world that slaves under and enslaves to greed.

As the reader will have noticed already, Alexander often used to feel cut off from this earth because of his ascetic disposition. It was precisely this disposition—love of God and of his fellow man—which, strangely enough, caused him to become a Jacobin, a friend of the oppressed and the suffering, and a friend of nature and all that belongs to it, great and small. For God also has His revolutions.

It was love for his neighbour that made him bury the widow at his own expense, be patient with poor tenants and overlook their debts, become their friend and suppress within himself the erroneous ideas that tried to hold him back from loving Pawlina, and rebel against the Order which was oppressing the Maltese.

Whenever society, distinguishing cruelly between one man and another, used to attack him because he would not surrender his principles, he often envisaged Christ walking, unseen, beside him and whispering: 'Be not afraid of my beloved poor, their tears and their sorrow will one day be your glory.' And it was for Christ that he had renounced the proud vanity of his mother and his family. He could never imagine Christ pointing to the portraits of his noble ancestors, but to the poor and to them that weep but believe, that thirst after justice and hunger for bread.

To preserve his principles sound and luminous, he never gave up reading the Holy Scriptures. From these he deduced the laws of life, and if these could not fit in with those of high society, he firmly held to them. He had learned by heart the Sermon on the Mount, that code of Christian morality, and whenever he read it he felt Christ to be alive, beholding Him in flesh and blood as though he were present among those who listened to His voice in the synagogues. There is so much to be digested in the Sermon on the Mount; read it, understand it, feel it, and there is one thing you will learn—that the world is still very far away from the Spirit of the Master. It is a world of wars, of men who do not bear one with the other, rich people without mercy, lukewarm characters who do no harm but also do no good, others who do good but also do much harm. It is a world where some die of over-eating while others die of want. Is this a Christian world? Where is that great sacrifice of man, in which he renounces himself completely? Some do: especially those whom the Church calls saints, and after them those whom the world calls philanthropists. But these are so few compared with the millions who live and die without ever having done any good. What a waste of lives, that pass away as if they had never existed!

So as to come nearer to Christ in deed and not in word only, Alexander felt that he had to stay far away from his family, from the halls decorated with silver chandeliers and portraits of barons, and to mingle with the poor, the ragged, the ill-treated. If these were mentioned with honour in Holy Scripture, what did it matter if society cast them aside? Whenever a man surrounds himself with vanity—so ran his argument—he will no more be able to understand his neighbour. What does a man who has abundance know of the distress of a father who cannot provide an evening meal for his children? What does he know? . . . What does he know? . . . How often does he awake in the night to reflect that another man like himself, a father as he is, is burying his head in his pillow to stifle his tears and sobbing so as not to let his wife and children hear him?

And it was because he feared that as long as he surrounded himself with vanities he could not love such people, feel for them and with them and understand them, that he detached himself from his family traditions, from the austere coldness of the pale faces of his ancestors, from the light-hearted follies of a highborn family, from balls, the playing of harpsichords and pianofortes, from singing and fondling soft damsels, from the society of stately, well-bosomed dames with pale painted lips and tired eyes, lashes smeared with eyeblack, from flattery, sarcasm, petting and caresses, lies, slander, and hypocrisy. Who is the king of this empty-headed people? Surely not He who spoke the Sermon on the Mount to a multitude thirsting after the word of life. Surely not He who came from the house of a carpenter, and passed His last dawn between two thieves.

His new friends were the pillars of the people of God: those clad in rags and tatters, the oppressed, beggars, widows, the sick, lepers, sinners, captives—all whose hearts were heavy with sorrow.

One of these friends of his was a blind old man called Nikol. He was poor and could not work for his living, yet he had been born with the right to feed himself no less than the monarch who rules over cities and men. That day, during the walk about which we have been speaking, Alexander found him seated on the threshold of his house, whiling away an hour all alone in the world of darkness which surrounded him. He had no one to take care of him, was wearing his only suit dirty all over, his trousers torn as there was nobody to patch them for him, his body bare for his shirt lacked buttons and revealed a hairy chest all filthy and sunburnt.

This poor blind man who saw nothing before him but darkness always yearned for someone to stop and have a chat with him; for he was always alone, and if nobody spoke to him he would hardly be conscious of being in the world at all.

As soon as Alexander saw the blind man his thoughts immediately returned to earth. 'Good morning, Nikol,' he greeted him.

'Good morning, my son,' answered the blind man. 'So you have come, my lover! Do talk to me whenever you are passing. Do talk to me, my son, and I shall pray for you. I'm always alone, my son, as I can see nobody, no one at all. Always speak to me, my son; I pray for everyone, but especially for those who speak to me.'

The blind man was dying for a conversation, and when he found someone to talk to he loosed his tongue. Alexander then asked, 'God's will be done; are you a bit downhearted, grand-dad?'

'I am, my son; but sometimes I console myself. Everyone has his cross to bear, my son; one man has one thing, one has another. Then you know what Dun Xand the Younger used to say, God have mercy on his soul: whoso suffers in this world will not be forgotten by God. And I believe him with all my heart. When death comes—and when it does come it will find you all the same, whether you are blind or not—it will deliver me from this life. So God's will be done.'

Alexander looked at the blind man with his extinguished eyes and asked himself, 'How did this old man come to shake off the dread of death, the thing that is most loathsome and terrifying to human instinct? Out of despair? But a man whose conversation is so tied up with the will of God cannot be said to lack hope. Then how was it?' Then a voice within him, the voice of his Christian conscience, answered: 'I, Christ, king of those who sorrow, give to my people the strength to suffer, and with it the strength not to fear death.'

Full of sympathy for that poor creature, Alexander sat down beside him and, just to pass the time away, asked: 'How many years do you count, granddad?'

'I count fourscore less three. In my time I have suffered much, my son, and before I became blind I worked hard. Sometimes I had to go to bed on an empty stomach whenever I found no work, especially when the corn ships came in late for unloading. Everything passes, though; and if I had lived in plenty wouldn't the time have passed by all the same, and wouldn't my age have been fourscore less three, and,' he added with a smile between his teeth yellow but all intact, 'after all, in the long run wouldn't the ball have hit the jack just the same?'

While the blind man was saying this he raised

himself slowly and rested his back against the projecting stone. So as not to let him think again of
past hardships Alexander changed the subject. 'Granddad, what are these projecting stones on either side
of the doorpost for?' he asked.

'They are there, my son, both as an ornament and
for a useful purpose. I remember, my son, during
some hard winters when we couldn't go out to draw
water from the well because of the storms, we used
to place buckets and even plates upon them and drink
the water that gathered in them.'

Then he added, 'Now, my son, it isn't that I want
to leave you, because it's a pleasure for me to chat
with you, but I must go inside to prepare my food.
Would you like to come in as well?'

'I won't keep you, grand-dad. But haven't you anybody to cook for you?'

'No, I've no one. My next door neighbour only
does the shopping for me.'

'Then how do you manage to do your cooking?'

'God gives one light according to one's circumstances, my son. Whenever I manage to get a penny
I buy some rice. A woman comes in to light the fire
and put the pot on it for me with some water. After
some time I pass my hand over the pot to see whether
it's boiling. If it is I close the palm of my hand in the
form of a funnel over the rim of the pot and pour the
rice into the water. When it has cooked I turn everything over, guided by my sense of touch.'

Alexander, reflecting sadly how much harder life is
for some people than for others, though the primary
rights to life are equal, put his hand into his pocket,

took out some gold sequins and placed them in the palm of the old man's hand.

'Here is some money, grand-dad, to help yourself with.'

'Are these sequins, my son? They're a real treasure-trove for me. You're just in time, for I spent my last farthings on rice today.'

The old man was greatly moved, and to show Alexander how much he appreciated his gift he begged him to let him kiss his hand. At first Alexander shuddered at the very thought of allowing his hands to touch the dirty, swollen lips of the blind man. But then he reflected that to refuse would be lack of due commiseration with the distress of a man of good will, so he overcame himself and gave his hand to him willingly. Then, seeing that the old man wanted to go inside but could not get up and walk alone, he helped him up and put his arms round his back, despite the fact that on such a blind old man the lice that breed in dirt might well not be lacking. He brought him in slowly, set him on his bed and, so as not to make him get up again, placed the pot on the fire with the meal handy to throw in.

The blind man was glad to see a youth like Alexander taking care of him as though he were his own father. 'My son,' he said again, 'whenever you pass by, do speak to me. After all, you always do. But do just speak to me, friend, even if you don't give me any charity. A blind man like me is always dying to find someone to have a chat with. And when you hear that I'm dead and you pass by this filthy place, say a requiem for me as well. See, it's all the same whether

I'm alive or dead for me, so long as God is with me.'

Alexander, marvelling at the blind man's saintly fortitude, thought within himself: 'Is there any revolution greater than that of faith, that peace may reign among men?'

When he had prepared everything for him, he bade him farewell, and left. But before quitting the neighbourhood he paid a visit to the woman who now and then dropped in on the blind man, and gave her some more money to buy him a new pair of trousers and a waistcoat, and to get hold of a man to give him a good wash all over.

As we have said above, between the Baroness and her son yawned a great gap which could not be bridged so easily.

She would have been inconsolable had she known what her son was doing at the time when the news her dear friend Baroness Klara brought her threw her into such a rage. If she had known that her son was nursing a blind, dirty, lousy old man! What would Biče have said, that doll with the dainty face, dainty lips, dainty ears, dainty mouth, dainty white hands, smooth slim legs white as snow, delicate bosom and sweet, spoilt voice? She would have abhorred the very idea that her brother was embracing a sightless old man. How she would have hidden her doll's face in her dainty hands, and told mama that she felt quite sick!

One marvels at the great difference that can exist between two minds, even if those two minds are derived from the same mother just as two fruits are produced from a single tree.

If the Baroness had really known what her son was doing, she would surely never have recovered from the shock, the faintness would have come upon her every time she thought of it.

On the other hand, Alexander knew nothing of what had occurred at their great residence. Little did he think that she who had brought him into the world, who had given him her milk without succeeding in transmitting to him her mind, was suffering a convulsion of thought and feeling, with a train of bitter thoughts passing through her brain.

And he returned to his own house as if nothing out of the ordinary had happened.

But as soon as he passed the threshold of the palace and saw Halwenija before him staring with red eyes as if she had been weeping, and weeping bitterly, he felt a shudder run through him.

He had a foreboding that something terrible must have happened in his own life and that of his mother. It is said that the heart's forebodings should be taken seriously, and Alexander felt all his senses gripped by deep anguish. He hesitated whether or not to go up, for he was afraid to know exactly what had taken place. But he plucked up courage and ran up to the room of his mother who had by now recovered, though she was still very faint. Halwenija hurried after him.

Beside his mother he found his sister Biċe. He loved his sister dearly, but truth to tell he did feel that this sister of his was just a human doll, brought up in the softness of aristocratic ease and unaware of any other world save that in which she had wandered ever since she saw the light, a world of vanity, balls, kisses, and playing of pianofortes. For that reason he had never opened his heart to her. It would have been impossible for her to understand him. She loved the pianoforte, but he loved the blind Nikol; she loved great gauds, but he loved charity. Biče had never allowed herself to be worried or concerned; but now, as soon as she saw her brother hurrying in between the lace curtains, she turned pale as if she felt a great misfortune descending upon her. She gave him a smile with lips that trembled, no more the smile of a doll but that of a sorrowful sister, as though to tell him that she had nothing against him, and that if she had never tried to understand him and help him in his ideas, at least she had never sought to cross his path, was never angry with him, reprimanded him, or prejudiced her mother against him.

When he saw his mother in that state he immediately felt a sense of guilt, and the sweat broke out on him. He felt guilty because of the look of accusation his mother gave him.

'What is wrong, mother?' he asked in a tremulous voice.

His sister Biče grew even paler. Alexander noticed it. The Baroness looked at him coldly, and a flush came into her angry countenance.

'Alexander,' she muttered (she did not call him 'my son', and he felt his blood freeze), 'Alexander, it is all your fault that I am in this state. . . . You will be the death of me. . . . You are dragging down the name of the family. . . . Your ancestors bequeathed to you a great name, a name of brave soldiers, and you do not care about it. . . . Instead of mixing with people of your own social class you go about with farmers, beggars, slaves, and widows. . . . You know that these are not your sort. . . . Some ladies have come into my home and put me to shame on your account. . . . Now you have even caused me to be whispered about. . . . You have debased me in the eyes of my own class. . . . I have had to hear that there has been some friendship between you and a peasant girl. I feel as if I am struck dumb. Who would have thought that the child I cherished and brought up with the greatest care should have turned into a useless man? And what of your sister? You know that she is engaged, and yet you have brought this dishonour upon her. Do you think that her betrothed will want to mix with a debased family? This is what has come of your books! A curse on them! A curse on your reading!' She stopped and sighed a moment, then asked in a firm voice, 'Is it true that you have lost your heart to a peasant girl?'

As she said this she sat up a little, her large staring eyes flashing below her white dishevelled hair, her lips pressed, the sweat shining on her forehead.

Alexander was touched at the sight of his mother's white hair, and felt an inward prompting to lie so as not to anger her. But his sensitive conscience revolted against this suggestion. 'By means of lies,' it warned him, 'you will not do anybody any good, neither yourself nor your mother.'

Torn between two conflicting feelings, the one battling to overcome the other, he lowered his head upon his breast and did not speak a word. In that silence the Baroness felt justified in reading the shame of a guilty man. Breathing rapidly, with her trembling hands plunged into her white hair, and with staring eyes, 'Alexander!' she shouted, 'you have eight days to think it over! Within eight days you must decide whether you want to ruin the mother who reared you. For eight days you must not set your eyes on me; and unless after that time you are prepared to tell me that there is nothing in this affair and that you intend to give up this company of yours, you must not count yourself as my son any longer, and get out of my house! I shall disown you and disinherit you.'

The Baroness—a poor victim of the twisted mentality of an aged society—was determined to give proof of the fierceness of a noble blood that is jealous of its honour even against the one she had loved so tenderly. But under the weight of this terrible threat which she would never retract, she again fell back fainting.

A cold shiver ran through Alexander's body, and in the intensity of his anguish tears streamed down his cheeks. For the very first time his sister Bičе, that lovely doll, appeared to have feelings; with tears in her eyes she threw her arms around him, embracing him and kissing him again and again. Bičе the pretty doll had been suddenly transformed into a sister who could feel, weep, and have compassion. Sorrow brings men more closely together.

Alexander too, amazed at this sudden change in his sister, embraced and kissed her and would not let her go. It was as though he sensed a high wall suddenly rising between them to separate them for ever.

His mother's threat had crushed him completely. But he felt no remorse, because he knew that it was not he who was responsible for reducing her to that state of misery, but her own prejudices. Neither he nor his mother was to blame; both he and she were victims. Who then was to blame? Who had exposed his mother's life to this hard trial? Who? None but Society with its unwritten code that a nobleman or a person of high rank ought not to mix with a low family.

The threat that he would be disinherited did not frighten him. He still had much property of his own, and even if he had not possessed anything, so long as he had a pair of hands he could work for his bread with the best of wills. But the threat that his mother, who had brought him up so fondly, who loved him and whom he loved so dearly, would disown him and turn him out of her house—it was this that shocked, dumbfounded, stupefied him.

Perplexed by the situation, he cast another tear-dimmed glance at her whom he thought of as having been done to death by the monster called Society, created by people who had never understood the simplicity of the Gospel; he glanced again at his sister, pale as death; then he hurried out to his own room. He was depressed and confused; he felt as though he had grown old suddenly, lifeless and without youthful vigour. In that moment he imagined the very light of the spirit to have been extinguished within him, and that he would never again return to his own.

In that moment, however, two familiar faces passed

before his eyes to cheer him—the face of the blind man Nikol with his burnt-out eyes, thanking and blessing him because he had given him to sup and bought him a suit; and Pawlina, like an angel with the serene countenance of one at prayer—he pictured this face going up to pray in a dark church where a flickering oil lamp burned before the Sacramental Christ, son of the Jewish carpenter.

Outside the door of his room, as he was fumbling to open it, with difficulty keeping on his feet, he found Halwenija waiting for him. He stood still. She looked beautiful but crushed; her eyes reflected the sad songs of her people as they journeyed across the vast expanses of sand; her lips were parted as if she was passionate to say something which she was too shy to utter. She was holding a silver candlestick with a candle in it, which trembled as if grasped in a feeble hand. He perceived that she was very much afraid, and that she was anxious about him. He gently patted her hair, the tears from his eyes running down into her large eyes, broken by a mortal grief. He placed his hand on her shoulder and spoke to her in a weak voice: 'Go to your room, and pray for me before the statuette of Our Lady of Sorrows which I bought you.'

She handed the candlestick to him and said in trembling accents, 'Yes, I shall pray for you before the Woman with the Pierced Heart.'

Within the angelic heart of this girl the peace of Christ was being born, for, God willing, Halwenija would soon be baptized. She bowed to him, smiled softly and went back to her room, her lips still parted as if wanting to say something but too shy to speak.

Locked up alone in his room Alexander, his hands clutching his hair, lay down on his bed and wept, pressing his face to the pillow to smother his sobs. His mother's threat to disown him had shattered him entirely. On the other hand he remained tied to his conscience and would not abandon those friends whom, illuminated by the inner spirit of the Gospel, he used to call Christ's own people.

He wept a long while; but at last, exhausted and worn out, he stretched himself on his bed to rest and forget. But at first he could not close his eyes, and when he did sleep, his sleep was as confused as that of a man in a high fever. He turned over from side to side without finding any rest, breathed deeply, threw away the bedding with his twisting, but all was in vain. Finally he slept, and dreamed a dream which he remembered all his life.

In the ravings of his broken sleep he had imagined that he heard Pawlina cry out to him tearfully because she thought that he had abandoned her; he saw his mother threatening him with those eyes staring with hatred which he had never seen before; he heard all over again the murmur of the conspiracy at Hal-Lija, the blind man Nikol blessing him, happy with the change of clothes he had brought him; the widow thanking him and promising to remember him in the next world; Halwenija sobbing and gazing at him with the sad black eyes of a child. It was out of this crazy mixture that his unforgettable dream was woven.

He saw himself walking into a very large palace,

decorated all about with crests and coats-of-arms. When he entered he felt thirsty, and thrust his hand into the water that was falling into a trough from a fountain and drank. When the water in the trough had settled he looked into it, and saw himself in rags. Suddenly he found himself surrounded by a crowd of tall men clad in armour, with pallid faces like skulls turning on a fleshless neck, their long bony fingers detached from their dry sockets, their sticks of legs stripped likewise of all flesh. They were like skeletons dressed up as soldiers. Suddenly a tongue of fire flashed forth, and someone with a voice that was not human cried out: 'Coward! . . .Coward! . . .' And those skeletons with bony fingers and sticks of legs put on flesh and walked towards him, their feet rattling inside their boots of steel. He recognized them. Those were the same faces, pale and hairy, which he knew from the portraits. His ancestors had risen from their graves to avenge themselves on him! At first they scowled at him, then they burst out laughing so loudly that their armour went on echoing their laughter even after it had ceased. And all of a sudden, like hungry vultures about to rend him apart they crowded round him, drew their swords and pressed in upon him with their pointed blades, while that inhuman voice cried incessantly: 'Coward! . . . Shame on you! . . . Shame on you! . . . Coward! . . .'

There was no one to defend him. Perhaps his mother . . . but there she was staring at him with cruel eyes as if she had never known him, as if he were not her son. He was alone. He broke into a sweat; he wanted to shout but could not utter a sound, as if numbed. Suddenly he feels himself free; his hand runs swiftly about his waist. He draws his dagger from its sheath, flourishes it above his head, and those pale faces draw back and vanish.

He woke up with a start, his hand still upon his thigh. Realizing that it was all a dream, he breathed deeply and felt relieved.

For him this dream meant that he had severed all bonds with his family once and for all. He sadly pressed his face against the pillows, and prayed to God that He might give him the strength and power to live without ever repenting of his convictions.

Ġ. AQUILINA

The Captain

CAPTAIN RAPHAEL was known to all Gozitans as a man who had sailed round half the world. He was a lively old fellow, affable, hearty, and never at a loss for a yarn. The young sailors of Mġarr, Għajnsielem, and Qala all swore by him; such was their high regard for him that they sought his advice on every problem that troubled them and relied on what he said.

Before the war you could usually see the Captain at Mġarr or Qala sitting on a bench outside a pub or squatting on a rock in the shade of a fishing-boat with a crowd of youths round him, telling them about his adventures when he was at sea. He had a very sharp tongue, knew plenty to say, and possessed the gift of enlarging on and embellishing a story so as to transform a thing of no account into a tale of wonder.

Captain Raphael had passed through many experiences during the half-century he had spent on the sea. At the age of eighteen he had embarked as a boy on a schooner, and he went on changing from one sailing ship to another, shuttling to and fro across the Mediterranean, until he became a boatswain. He then signed on and embarked in a cargo boat, sailed to England, and from there to the greatest ports in the whole world, visiting far-off lands. In the course of his travels he had come across people of all colours and races, and learned of strange customs which he had never even dreamed of before. He took up all sorts of jobs, and sometimes found himself in plenty of trouble, but this only helped to open his eyes and teach him what the world had to offer. Finally in his old age, ripe in years, weary of travelling around and with a mind full of the wisdom of life, he returned to his native land to seek repose in the friendship of his fellow countrymen and in the peace and blessing of his own home.

When the Captain finally cast anchor at Għajnsielem the friends of his childhood gathered round him, and in a short time he became the best known and most beloved character in the neighbourhood. He was a fine figure of a man, tall and straight as a beam; his face was wrinkled, and his blue eyes sparkled under the peak of his service cap; his teeth were still sound and white, and his thick lips were always parted in a cheerful smile; but above all he had a mane that was recognizable a mile off, for the hair of his head, eyebrows, and moustache was as white as snow, which gave him the appearance of a wise and prudent man.

Raphael was a friend to all, and mixed with everyone who spoke to him. Nothing could ever annoy or offend him, but he did not like it if people failed to address him as Captain. Nobody knew for sure whether Captain Raphael had ever actually been in command of a big ship, a schooner, or even some small vessel; but he fancied himself as a captain, and wanted everyone to treat him as such. His word was law, and he would not allow anyone to question any pronouncement of his on matters connected with the sea.

When the war broke out, his friends tried to

persuade him to sail again, and somebody spread the rumour that he was about to be commissioned in the Navy. But Raphael would not hear of joining up except as a captain.

Between one air-raid and another Captain Raphael was to be seen at Mġarr giving advice to a group of ferrymen gathered round him on how to avoid mines, how to make use of sheltering rocks, or how to escape from enemy aircraft. All night he could be seen with a crowd about him in the corner of an air-raid shelter, narrating his adventures in the wars he had been through in his lifetime.

As time passed the enemy attacks became much heavier. The air-raids went on without intermission; there was hardly time to breathe between one attack and the next. Everyone took cover as best he could, and did his work in the shortest possible time so as to avoid remaining long in the open, as enemy aircraft hovered overhead continually, often diving down to sow destruction with their fire.

The crews of the Gozo boats were in great danger. The enemy planes had taken to hunting these craft as they plied between the two islands, and shot them up until they made them look like sieves with their machine-gun bullets. Many sailors were killed, many others were gravely wounded, and so many of the boats were sunk that hardly any more remained to sail between Malta and Gozo. Although most of the sailors had been wiped out, the few who remained did not neglect their duty, and with amazing courage continued to transport the produce, goods, and harvest from Gozo to Malta.

In Malta itself there was great misery, and many people suffered from hunger; thus the cargoes of the Gozo boats were of no small value for keeping up the morale of the Maltese and encouraging them to hold out. But in the end the attacks became so fierce and the destruction of the craft so thorough, that there were hardly any boats or sailors left to carry on the service between Malta and Gozo.

Among the vessels remaining afloat was an old ship that had first touched water in the days of Queen Victoria. After having changed hands many times and carried all sorts of cargoes, she had finally entered our harbour and there remained, grazing alongside the jetty. She was a small steamship, begrimed with rust and smoke, ponderous as could be, but quite capable of facing the heaviest seas.

When the Gozo boats became fewer and fewer, this steamer was called in to transport passengers, food, and mail between the two islands. On account of the shortage of coal she was only able to make the crossing every other day, and each time ran into some trouble or other; sometimes she would receive a hail of bullets from the aircraft, or she would almost collide with a floating mine, or else she would pick up some fishermen whose boat had just been sunk by the enemy.

During one of these trips between Malta and Gozo, as the ship was nearing the small island of Comino a formation of enemy planes attacked her, and wounded the commander so badly that when she anchored alongside the wharf at Mġarr she was without a captain.

Among the letters that the ship had brought that

day was one for Clara, Captain Raphael's sister. It was a service letter, and as soon as Clara saw it she became alarmed and her heart throbbed with fear.

Captain Raphael's sister was a widow. She had only one son who had been called up for military service. Day and night she thought about him, her heart palpitating with anxiety, always expecting to receive bad news about him. Captain Raphael, who lived with his sister, used to calm her as best he could, trying his utmost to drive these ugly thoughts out of her mind. But nothing could bring comfort to the fond mother, who would often pass the whole night thinking and talking of her son. During an air-raid on Malta, as from the roof of her house she watched the enemy planes diving, the shells bursting, the smoke of the guns and the dust clouds of exploding bombs, the Captain's sister used to visualize her son working hard at his gun, expecting him to be carried away to the next world by a bullet at any moment.

Clara did not have the courage to open the letter; it was as though she had a foreboding of the bad news it contained. She therefore called her brother to read it to her. Captain Raphael opened the letter with a smile on his lips but with trembling hands, and at the first glance read the sad tidings which he had always anticipated. In one of the heavy raids on Malta Clara's son had been gravely wounded; he had been taken to St. Andrew's Hospital where he lay in a delirium all the time, calling for his mother. The doctor wished Clara to come and see her son, if only to satisfy his longing and to calm him; her visit might also do him good, and help him to recover.

Clara wanted to leave for Malta immediately, but how could she get there? There were no boats to make the crossing, and the steamer had no captain. The poor mother almost went out of her mind; she ran along the streets crying and screaming, went down to Mġarr begging to be ferried over, and could scarcely keep from jumping into the water to swim across or be drowned. Her desperation brought tears to the eyes of all who saw her, but it was all in vain; she had to go back to Għajnsielem with a broken heart and wait till the morrow, when perhaps somebody might possibly leave Gozo for Malta and take her over with him.

But God consoles man in all the afflictions that may visit him. That evening while Clara, surrounded by her neighbours, was immersed in a sea of sorrows, even Captain Raphael not knowing what to do with himself, a police inspector arrived from Rabat who wished to speak with the Captain.

'Captain Raphael,' said the inspector, 'the Island Commissioner has sent me to look for you.'

'What's wrong?' asked the Captain in astonishment.

The inspector, who had heard about the sad news which Clara had received, immediately answered.

'The Commissioner requires of you a service which will be of the greatest help to the country.'

'What?' asked the Captain, amazed.

'The mail boat came in this morning with its captain badly wounded, and if no one is found to take charge of it, it will remain tied up to the wharf. Now there is a cargo of foodstuffs that is very much needed in Malta. If it remains here it will go bad. Besides, there are many people who are awaited in Malta for digging shelters; but above all, the Commissioner wants to send some very important letters to the Government. He would therefore like to entrust you, as captain, with the mail boat, to take it to Malta tomorrow.'

The Captain's heart filled with joy. He felt flattered to know that, though he was old and tired, his services were still required by his country. He had very often wished that he was still young enough to make his contribution towards the well-being and deliverance of his homeland. Now he found himself actually called upon by the Head of the State to perform a task which no one else but he could accomplish. The thought that he was about to have a ship to command encouraged him, and he experienced an incomparable joy on finding himself commissioned as captain. It was true that he had not been put in command of a man-o'-war, but the little steamer which had been entrusted to him was in the service of the state, and he, as captain, felt that he was in the service of the King.

Captain Raphael went in to comfort and encourage his sister by promising her to take her to Malta on the morrow. That night he could hardly close his eyes, and very early next morning he hastened down to Mġarr, and climbed aboard to take command of the vessel. As soon as he felt the ship rocking gently under his feet, inhaled the sea air, and felt the morning breeze on his face, Captain Raphael was instantly rejuvenated, imagining himself to be in the prime of his youth. He immediately began giving orders, posting the sailors to their various duties and seeing that everything was ship-shape. He peeped down into the engine room, gave a couple of turns to the helm, inspected the compass, and made the rounds of the whole ship. At the same time the cargo began to be loaded aboard, and after a while the passengers arrived. Clara was one of the first. Under her faldetta she carried a bunch of flowers which she had picked for her son from her own pot. At sunrise the mail bags were brought in. The moorings were loosened. The ship heaved, and set out for Malta.

It was a lovely morning, bright and sunny. The sea hardly moved at all, and the fields and rocks around had a calm, serene look as if drowsing in the slumber of benediction and peace.

The small ship sailed on in the lee of Comino, past Fliegu, towards Mellieħa Bay, below Selmun Tower, on to the small islands at St. Paul's, and advanced towards Salini. The passengers, who had been nervous when they left Gozo for fear of enemy aircraft, plucked up courage the nearer they came to Valletta, and though all of them were constantly glancing at the sky many nourished high hopes of ending the voyage without incident.

As they were sailing past Baħar-iċ-Ċagħaq Captain Raphael, who had been on the look-out for anything unusual, suddenly sighted a soldier on Magdalene Tower waving a red flag. The Captain was startled but not alarmed, as he had all the time been expecting that signal, indicating an air-raid. Without appearing in the least perturbed or confused, he ordered one of his men to run up a red flag to the mast-head as a signal to the soldiers that he had understood their warning. He then went on deck, gathered all the passengers into a cabin below the bridge, told them that enemy air-craft were attacking Malta, and asked them not to panic. He cheered them up, but warned them not to expose themselves on deck, and added a couple of words of comfort to his sister.

As soon as he had freed himself from the passengers Captain Raphael went up again on the bridge, took a deep breath, grasped the wheel firmly, and stamped his feet on the planks below him. If anyone could have seen the Captain at that moment, they would have been astonished at the fierceness of his mien. His eyes shone and sparkled like a falcon's. His pursed lips, his wrinkled forehead, the peak of his cap drawn side-ways over his eyebrows, all gave the impression of a man absorbed in strong determination, a will that feared neither trial nor death.

A couple of shots were heard, and the drone of aeroplane engines filled the air. All of a sudden Cap-tain Raphael, who had been watching the sky like a hawk, perceived a formation of enemy planes coming towards him like hungry vultures swooping upon their prey. The Captain gave a couple of quick turns to the wheel. The ship suddenly leaped, leaned over on its side, and veered sharply to the right. The wheel then turned in the opposite direction and the ship changed course to the left. Thus they went on, with the ship zigzagging rapidly to confuse the aim of the aircraft. The latter lost no time but quickly began to hurl their deadly bombs, which raised mountains of water around the little ship wherever they fell. But the ship, steered with great skill by her captain, slipped clear of every peril. She shook and leaped at every bomb that exploded but went on, gliding to the left and the right like a sea-gull on the surface of the water.

The enemy pilots were furious to see that they could not cope with that nutshell of a ship. They had expected to shatter it with the first couple of bombs, and they felt foiled and humiliated by the tiny vessel. They were in a rage of indignation, and when they saw that they could not stove it in with their heavy bombs they began to dive down and sweep it with machine-gun fire.

The first warplane took the lead. It heeled sideways, dived down upon the ship, and as soon as it was near enough opened fire with all its guns. The leader was followed by the second and third planes, then by the others until all of them had had a try. The ship kept on zigzagging, but the bullets began to rain down upon her, and in a short time they made a sieve of her. Some of the passengers were wounded, and a great panic ensued. The whistling of the bullets, the noise they made when they hit the steel plates, the smashing of the furniture, the breaking of the glass, together with the groans of the wounded, the shouts of the men, the screams of the women and the crying of the children, above all the whine of the diving planes, created a fearful uproar.

All of a sudden one aircraft screamed down to mast height, firing like a demon. Straightway Captain Raphael yelped with pain and toppled down to the deck, pressing his hands against his chest which crimsoned with blood.

As soon as the Captain fell wounded the ship lost

way and floated out of control, like a leaf swimming on the surface of the water. That was the time to finish it off once for all. Had the enemy planes just dropped one bomb on it they would have blown it to pieces; but at that moment their attention was diverted elsewhere: a formation of Spitfires had swooped down upon them, routed them, and wreaked havoc among them.

Nevertheless the ship was badly holed, and began to leak; in a short time it listed so dangerously that there was a risk it would capsize entirely and drown all who were aboard. The passengers quickly realized what danger they were in and were scared out of their wits; almost frantic with fear, they ran shouting hither and thither in complete despair, creating the utmost confusion.

This confusion multiplied the danger, and a great disaster was imminent. But Captain Raphael though gravely wounded had not forgotten his ship. He called one of the sailors to help him to his feet and hold him up, and while he grasped the wheel in his hands he made signal for full speed ahead.

Water had flooded the holds, and the ship was weighed down. Doubled up with pain, and with death in his eyes, the Captain threw his whole weight on the wheel and turned it round until the ship's prow faced the nearest point of the coast, the rocks beneath St. Andrew's. It was a race between the water which gushed into the hold and the ship steaming towards land. The lives of all on board hung on that race; if the ship made it and ran aground there was a chance for the passengers to be saved, but if the water that flooded the hold sank the ship many of them would go down with it.

All on board felt their blood freezing. Many began to pray for help from God and to make vows to Our Lady of Pinu; others burst into heart-rending screams. Some embraced their children, while others prepared to swim to the shore. Clara was heart-broken with grief. She climbed up to the bridge near her brother, but when she saw his face pale as death and his chest covered with blood she almost fainted. She was on the point of collapse; but suddenly she overcame her dizziness and hurried eagerly to the side of the sailor who was holding up the Captain, to give him a hand and look after her brother. But her brother had lost too much blood, and after a while he collapsed.

As time went on the ship sank steadily, and the waves were already washing the decks and were about to engulf the whole ship. Then all of a sudden a crunch was heard, followed by a tearing and a bumping under water. The ship stopped at once and came to rest on the rocks beneath St. Andrew's Hospital, where many soldiers were waiting to give help to the passengers.

The Commanding Officer of the hospital, together with other officers who had witnessed the attack of the enemy planes upon the small ship and marvelled at the dexterity and skill the Captain had shown to escape from the aircraft and from sinking, immediately sent medical supplies and other necessities to aid the wounded.

In a short time the passengers were brought ashore and taken to the hospital. The wounded were kept there; the rest, after receiving some refreshment to overcome their fright, were sent home. Captain Raphael was carried into a ward and tended with great care, so that after a short while he showed signs of recovery and regained consciousness. As soon as he opened his eyes he looked round to see where he was. When he cast his gaze upon the bed next to him he started with joy; he felt greatly relieved, and the blood flushed back into his face, covered as it was with sweat and colourless as that of a man in the last agony. At first the Captain could hardly believe his eyes, and closed them once more, but after a time he reopened them and moved to look at the bed beside him. The English nurse very gently helped him up, and the Captain parted his lips in a smile of joy on seeing in the bed next to his Clara's son holding his mother's hand and gazing at her with a look that carried his heart with it. Clara's eyes were wet with tears, and though they reflected grief at the fate which had befallen her brother, the Captain perceived in those sorrowful eyes a spark of joy kindled by the reunion of a mother with her son.

At that moment the colonel with his staff came up to the bed, and after saluting Captain Raphael in the military fashion he clasped his hand and congratulated him on having by his skill saved the ship from the bombs and the passengers from drowning. After praising the courage he had shown, he promised that he would send in a report that due recognition might be shown to the Captain.

Raphael parted his lips in a smile of gratitude. In his heart of hearts he had always desired to pass as a captain. Now he saw the fulfilment of that wish, and rejoiced in that moment of fame and glory. At the end of his life he had the great fortune of seeing himself honoured as a famous captain, surrounded by colonels and other officers, all singing the praises of his deeds. He almost swooned with the joy that shone forth through his eyes as he looked at Clara and her son. One of the officers approached the colonel and told him that Clara was the Captain's sister. On hearing this the colonel also shook Clara by the hand and congratulated her on her son's recovery. As soon as the Captain heard this he experienced a great joy, for he understood that the trip which his sister had made from Gozo was not in vain.

Having stayed there for some time, the colonel before leaving again shook Captain Raphael by the hand, but the latter was now so weak that he hardly had strength enough to thank him. Before the colonel departed he gave orders that everything possible should be done to save the Captain's life.

But the Captain's life had reached its end. Sadly and in silence he closed his eyes, awaiting his Creator to call him to eternal life. That man of the sea, who had seen half the world, who had drunk of the sweetness and the bitterness of life, who had passed through great tribulation, having discharged his last duty now found himself at rest. He had done his duty towards his homeland, and done it like a man. He had been commissioned to take the ship, mail, cargo, and passengers to Malta, and by hook or by crook he had done so. He had succeeded in taking his sister to the bedside of her son, who was now on the mend. He had received praise and honour from a high-ranking officer, and his name would be remembered with glory. Now it was finished, and Captain Raphael surrendered himself into the hands of Jesus.

The next morning Captain Raphael was buried. He was given the honours of a naval captain, carried on a gun-carriage between two ranks of sailors. They covered him with the White Ensign and laid upon him the bunch of flowers which Clara had brought from Gozo. Behind the hearse walked naval captains, colonels, and officers.

Ġ. GALEA

The Bet

THE main characters in our story were two old people,
husband and wife, who were well known in the village
for three reasons—firstly because they were the oldest
married couple in the place; secondly because they
were the most frequent church-goers—indeed they
were to be seen waiting at the door of the church
before opening time summer and winter alike, in fair
weather and foul, they heard all the Masses from
beginning to end, always walked piously after the
priest carrying the viaticum, took part in every procession, and listened to all the sermons; and thirdly
because in spite of all this, and in spite of the fact that
they still loved each other like a newly married couple,
they quarrelled over the merest trifles and raged at
one another for the slightest thing. Not once or twice
already the bigwigs of the village, the parish priest or
the chemist, had played some trick on them to trigger
them off, as when the chemist one day found Rozi at
the door and asked her:

'What did you have for lunch today, Roz? What an
appetizing smell!'

'Oh, nothing much, sir,' Rozi answered. 'I cooked
some octopus stew.'

'What!' said the chemist. 'Is it you who do the
cooking?'

'Of course it's me. Who else should it be but me?'

'As a matter of fact,' the chemist said, 'your Wenzu

was saying in my dispensary that it's he who prepared the stew.'

And when Wenzu came home. . . . There was nothing she didn't say and do to him.

But let's pass on to our story.

It was the night between Holy Saturday and Easter Sunday, and Wenzu had stayed a bit longer than his habit in Kurun's pub, jabbering with his friend the chemist and other cronies. When he walked back home—this is between ourselves—he was well accompanied, because he had taken a few drops more than usual. He opened the door and entered to find Rozi already huddled up in her bed. As quick as knife he had pulled off his clothes, thrown himself down on his bed in another corner of the same room, and dropped off to sleep immediately.

But poor chap, he didn't enjoy his sleep for long.

'Wenz,' he heard a voice saying, 'Wenz, is that the way you do things? Do you get into bed without even closing the outside door?'

Without saying a word Wenzu poked his head up from under the blanket, and as their house consisted of only two rooms, one behind the other, he perceived that he really had left the street door open.

Rozi, who had seen him peep out, and had also noticed by his red face that that evening the wine had done its work, said in a voice which women can use to cut you through without a knife:

'You red-eyed tunny this evening! Come on, get up and close the door, you drunkard!'

That was exactly what Wenzu needed to feel the full effect of the wine. He almost got out of his bed to argue the point with his wife, but he felt the cold and got in again.

'Well, aren't you going to shut the door?' Rozi asked.

'Go and shut it yourself,' answered Wenzu promptly.

'See me going,' said Rozi. 'Aren't you ashamed of yourself, to say that to a woman my age, who slaves after you from morning to night?'

'Well, if you're old, am I a young man?' Wenzu said. 'And haven't I been at work since dawn?'

'Don't talk rubbish,' answered Rozi. 'Come on, get up and close the door. It was you who left it open and it's you who must shut it.'

'Not me!' said Wenzu. 'What if I catch cold, will you cure me?'

'Well, what shall we do?'

'What do you want us to do? We'll sleep with the door open. We're poor people. We've nothing to steal.'

'But I don't want to sleep with the door open,' Rozi began to wail.

'Well then, go and shut it.'

'That I won't do. You go, you lazy drunkard.'

Wenzu was about to get up again, but he thought better of it. He turned towards his wife and said:

'I tell you what we'll do. The first one of us who says a word will have to get up and shut the door. Agreed?'

'Agreed!' answered Rozi.

Wenzu turned on one side, Rozi turned on the other, and immediately there was dead silence. Privately Wenzu congratulated himself on having invented this splendid idea; and he fell asleep again.

But Rozi could not close her eyes. The thought that the door was still open made her uneasy. The little oil lamp flickering on its shelf in front of the statuette of the Madonna began to get on her nerves. She turned this way and that in her bed, but it was all in vain. A hundred times she was on the point of opening her mouth to give Wenzu a piece of her mind. But each time she remembered that whoever spoke first would have to get up and close the door, and she kept a rein on her tongue if only to spite him, and so remained silent. All of a sudden she heard footsteps in the street outside. They came nearer and nearer. As soon as they reached the door they stopped.

Rozi pricked up her ears and stared with bulging eyes. What should she do? Should she wake up Wenzu? That was out of the question; it would only make her lose the bet, and she would rather die than surrender.

Who was the person standing at the door?

It was the chemist. Having filled himself with wine to his heart's content he was walking home slowly, when on passing his friend Wenzu's house he noticed that the door was open. He stopped, looked in, and saw the flickering light of the oil lamp. What was all this? Was Wenzu going mad? Was it possible that they could sleep with the door open? And Rozi, where was she?

He called softly: 'Wenz.'

No answer. He called again:

'Roz.'

Again no answer. He lifted his voice a little:

'Wenz.'

Perfect silence.

In the meantime Wenzu had woken up as well, and was just about to answer when he suddenly remembered the bet and covered his mouth with the blanket.

The chemist began to get worried. What with seeing something so out of the way, and what with the wine doing its work on him, he started shouting:

'Wenz, Roz, are you dead?'

He went in, and saw both Rozi and Wenzu lying on their beds, fast asleep.

He walked up to Wenzu:

'Come on, Wenz, get up. Your door's open. What's all this?'

But Wenzu was as immovable as a stone. The chemist turned to Rozi.

'Get up, Rozi. Come on, Roz, Roz, Wenz, Wenz. My God, they're both dead!'

And he ran off as fast as his legs could carry him to the house of the parish priest. When he arrived he was out of breath. He rang the bell.

'What's wrong? Who is there?' answered the priest inside.

'Come quickly, Father. Wenzu and Rozi are both dead.'

'Just a moment,' said the parish priest. He quickly put on his clothes and started walking with the chemist towards Wenzu's home. As they passed the doctor's house they called him out as well. Some people on their way home asked what was the matter, and in a flash the news spread through the whole village that Wenzu and Rozi had both died at the same instant.

'Poor dears,' said some. 'They loved one another

so much while they were alive that they died together.'

Others said: 'Well, anyhow, they won't quarrel any more now.'

So, along with the chemist, the doctor, and the parish priest, half the village gathered in Wenzu and Rozi's house. They were all looking at them, some with tears in their eyes. The two of them remained silent, lying on their backs with never a sign of life. The doctor went up to both of them in turn and felt their pulses.

'They're still alive,' he said. 'Father, you give them Extreme Unction while I go back home to fetch some medicine to bring them round, because it looks as if they're both in extremis.'

While the parish priest was putting on his surplice, which he had brought along just in case, everybody knelt down, made the sign of the cross, and began reciting the litany of the dying. The priest approached Wenzu.

'Wenz,' he said, 'can you hear me?'

No answer.

'Roz, are you able to hear me?'

Also no answer. He might just as well have addressed the wall. So he turned back to Wenzu and said:

'Wenz, if you can hear me but cannot answer make an act of contrition, because I am about to anoint you.'

But at this point an odd thing happened. For when the priest uncovered Wenzu's feet to make ready for the anointing, and felt them to see whether they were cold, Wenzu couldn't stand it any longer as he was very ticklish in that spot. He sat up on the bed and cried breathlessly: 'Oh, Father, you're tickling me!'

Immediately Rozi sat up in the other bed and cried:

'See, I've had my way. Now then, you drunkard, get up and shut the door.'

Ġ. ZAMMIT

The Museum Mystery

THE Commissioner had not been mistaken. His reputation as well as his job were now balanced on the edge of a steep precipice, especially after the amazing robbery which had taken place in August of that same year inside the Malta Museum, during an important visit of a French parliamentary delegation on its way home from North Africa.

The delegation even included two Ministers, and one can imagine what a splendid reception they were given in Malta despite the fact that they were travelling incognito.

They were invited to tea-parties, dinners, balls, and of course among the places they visited were the Post Office building, the Palace Armoury, and the Museum.

At the Post Office there was nothing special to see, though they were very interested in the marble plaque on the façade commemorating the fact that Napoleon Bonaparte chose that building as his residence during his stay in Malta.

Afterwards they went to the Museum, which is across the road from the Post Office. Their visit here, in contrast to the preceding one, was rather prolonged.

Our Museum is not large, and cannot be compared with the great museums of the world, especially the Louvre in Paris. But for its size it contains many objects well worth seeing, much more than might be supposed, as the French delegation proved by spending more than two hours visiting the place. Among the articles preserved there, they took a special interest in the collection of coins donated to Malta by Pisani. This collection is a really splendid one, and it attracted the attention not only of the visitors but also of the Maltese who were showing them round and keeping them company. Many of the latter had never given any heed to that treasure before. But that is the usual way things happen; when something is close at hand we take no notice of it, but if anything is far away we wish it were among us.

Among the Maltese present was the flower of Maltese society—nobles, heads of Government departments, one of the Bishop's chaplains, the Presidents of the Chambers of Advocates, doctors, businessmen, and others. It seemed that never had there been assembled outside the Museum such a long line of cars as on that day.

Mr. Frank Gatt the Commissioner, both on account of his social standing and because his wife was French and belonged to one of the best families, was among the most conspicuous persons in the group. His wife Madame Lucie let her tongue wag properly when she found herself . . . in her own environment and with people of her own race.

The Commissioner's secretary too played an important part in the gathering, as his chief had asked him to act as guide and interpreter in St. John's Cocathedral, the Armoury, &c. But at the Museum Madame Lucie took over personally, asking one of the high officials of the Museum, who spoke French as well as she did, to help her on some points. For this reason Mr. Gatt's secretary had remained in the Commissioner's car with Baskal, the new chauffeur who had taken Loreto's place.

As we have already observed, what pleased the delegation most was the collection of old coins donated by Pisani, around which they crowded like flies about a honey-pot, listening to Madame Gatt as she explained each section, turning round to the Museum officer whenever she got stuck and whispering in Maltese, 'You carry on now.'

Bendu Muscat, the secretary, had not undertaken the job of guide and interpreter without a good reason. In his mind he had other motives than simply to obey his chief, to cut a handsome figure, and to make propaganda for Malta: he wanted to keep an eye on all those places where high society gathered, during which occasions the many mysterious robberies had occurred.

Another thing: Madame Lucie had been accustomed of late to attend these parties all alone, as Mr. Gatt had begun to loathe them, because whenever a robbery took place at a party where the Police Commissioner happened to be present the newspapers would make capital out of it, and had quite a few things to say on the subject. So Mr. Gatt had asked his secretary to take care of his wife whenever he was able to accompany her.

Bendu did not refuse for various reasons. First of all he did not like to displease his chief; secondly, as secretary he felt it his duty to make friends with the chauffeur, to see what kind of a man he was, who his associates were, his habits, and whether he could be trusted with Madame Lucie; and thirdly—and this was his strongest reason—because he was angling for . . . a big fish. It was therefore the most natural thing in the world that on the day of the French parliamentarians' visit he too was there beside the driver to act as guide; but his secret intentions were quite other.

Meanwhile, in the great hall of the Museum above a fine inquisition was in progress. For to the series of mysterious thefts yet another, perhaps the greatest of them all, had been added—an amazing theft which would have evil consequences for a number of people: the Director of the Museum, the officer who was acting as guide, the head of that section of the Museum, and the Commissioner of Police.

What had happened then, to cause all this?

Among the Frenchmen was M. Gastou, one of the Directors of the Louvre, who had taken a particular interest in the coin collection and examined each coin with a magnifying glass, because, as he said, there were some that had very great value, there being few similar ones in the whole world.

As everyone knows, the collection is kept in glass cases shaped like small tables, and it is not easy to examine each individual coin minutely while it is still in the case. It was for this reason that Madame Lucie, seeing that M. Gastou was taking so much interest in the coins and straining his eyes, asked the man in charge if he could open the case so that the Frenchman could give his expert opinion on those precious coins which constituted such an ornament to the Malta Museum.

The man hesitated for a moment; but Madame Lucie begged him not to lose such an opportunity, which might not occur again for goodness knows how long. The man was reluctant to disappoint her, and was also very anxious to learn something new about the collection. So he went up to the head of the section to obtain the requisite permission, and as soon as this was granted he opened the case and placed it at the disposal of the great French expert.

Thereupon many people began to crowd round him asking him various questions which he answered, distributing the desired information with the greatest ease. In a flash, six or seven more magnifying glasses appeared and the finest of the coins—some four or five —began to circulate from hand to hand and were examined with the greatest care. Many of the Maltese present, who had never shown any interest in such beautiful things, listened with the closest attention to the words of M. Gastou and a couple of other experts.

You can imagine Madame Lucie in these circumstances giving the most careful explanations, using choice words which could not be understood by anyone who was not French, and translating into Maltese what M. Gastou was saying for the benefit of some present.

After about half an hour, when everyone had returned what was in his hand to the head of the section, who from the moment the case had been opened had not moved from that place, and when he had put them back in the case one by one, he noticed that one coin was missing. Meanwhile, however, many of the visitors had already left the hall.

'Il en manque une . . . il en manque . . . ' he began telling them in a rather high-pitched voice. But nobody took any notice, either because they could not hear or because they could not understand.

Now all the people had left that room and were spreading about in the other rooms. He therefore locked the door of the hall and ran like mad to the Director of the Museum who at that moment was inside his office.

As soon as the Director heard the quite unexpected bad news and was told of the mysterious way in which the coin had disappeared, he flushed with confusion and had to take hold of the first chair he could find so as not to collapse. He then turned as pale as a lemon.

What steps could be taken against so many people who filled the Museum, especially if one considered that those gentlemen were among the best people in Malta, each better known than the other so that one could hardly tell who was the most distinguished among them? The least suspicion would have been interpreted by them as the deepest insult. On the other hand if he failed to take the necessary steps that very instant, while the stolen coin was still inside somewhere, what a fix he would find himself in! What excuse could he give when accused of letting the thief slip through his very fingers?

What could he possibly do? Every moment was worth its weight in gold.

'Wait here,' he told the man, and ran breathlessly to the entrance of the Museum. When he arrived there he asked the ticket seller who was watching at the door with the porter:

'Tell me, has anyone gone out during the last five minutes?'

'No, sir, no one. But why do you ask? You're looking very strange!'

'Nothing . . . nothing . . . . But do me a favour. Go and look for Mr. Gatt among the gentlemen who are visiting the Museum and tell him I need him at once, and that I'm waiting down here for him—as quick as possible. Do you understand? The Commissioner Mr. Gatt.'

'Yes . . . yes . . . .'

'You know him, don't you?'

'Of course I do. Isn't he the Police Commissioner?'

'That's him. Run!'

After two minutes the ticket seller came back with the Commissioner hurrying a short distance behind him. When he saw the disturbed look on the Director's face his heart missed a beat.

'Well now, what's wrong?'

The Director drew him aside, and between breaths —for he was blowing like a runaway bull—told him in a few words what had happened.

'I was expecting some unpleasant incident,' said Mr. Gatt with a bit of a stammer. 'But not as bad as this.' After a few seconds he went on. 'Wait. . . . Wait for me here . . . just one minute. . . . But don't let anyone pass beyond this threshold.'

And he ran out into the street, leaving the Director waiting there in suspense.

'Where is the Commissioner going? Who to?' mused the Director in astonishment. 'And why did he go out when I told him plainly that nobody had yet stepped outside the threshold and that the thief, or rather the thieves, were still inside the Museum?'

He had no time for further thoughts, because Mr. Gatt reappeared accompanied by a rather short and weak-looking man, who did not inspire much confidence. This man was Bendu Muscat!

'Mr. Muscat, may I introduce you to the Director of the Museum, whom I presume you already know, as you like to ramble about in interesting corners. But let's come to the point, as there isn't much time to lose. He'll tell you in a couple of words what's happened during the past ten minutes. If some of the people inside manage to walk out of this place, everything will be lost for us, and as you very well know the consequences will be bad, dreadful. On the other hand, all the people in here are high-ranking persons. What do you advise, Mr. Muscat? What's to be done?'

So as not to lose any time, while the Director was informing Mr. Muscat of what had happened and of the great value of the stolen coin, Mr. Gatt went off into the corridor that faces the main entrance to see what had happened to the visitors.

'Very well,' said Mr. Muscat to the Director in the coldest of tones, after listening to everything without so much as batting an eyelid.

He then turned to Mr. Gatt who had rejoined them, and said to him:

'Mr. Gatt, with your permission I would like a word with you in private.'

The Commissioner, who had completely lost his head, immediately stepped aside as soon as he heard Bendu talking to him and left the Director standing there all alone. Mr. Gatt had taken to Bendu from their very first meeting, as we have already made clear, but after the affair of the chauffeur Loreto he had placed all his confidence in him. Mr. Muscat noticed immediately that the Director looked a little offended, and not wishing to lose his help over such a trifle he turned to him and said:

'Do please join us, sir. There are no secrets from you.'

But Bendu's words were just empty compliments, for he never entrusted his secrets to anybody . . . anybody at all . . . to himself alone . . . for he always thought that a secret shared, even with one other person, was no longer a secret.

As soon as the three of them were gathered together behind the main door he told them briefly:

'Who besides ourselves knows about this theft?'

'As far as I know,' the Director answered at once, 'only the man in charge of the section and . . .' the Director stopped for a moment to take a deep breath, 'the blasted thief.'

Bendu interrupted him, for there was no time to be lost.

'Well, do me a favour, go and call the man here. But quick, because I hear footsteps, and I'm afraid the visitors are already leaving.'

'I'll do so immediately,' answered the Director as though Bendu were his superior. And he went off, almost at a run, to carry out his orders without waste of time. When he was gone the Commissioner asked his secretary:

'Mr. Muscat, please don't leave me on tenterhooks.

What are your plans? A general search of everyone before they go out, eh?'

'What are you saying, sir? You forget who you're dealing with. Nothing of the sort; in fact, I'm letting them all go without even informing them of what has happened, because . . . . '

He had not finished his sentence when the Director arrived with the man in charge of Pisani Hall—for that was the name by which the person was known who had special charge of the section where was preserved the collection of ancient and other coins bequeathed by Mr. Pisani to the Malta Museum.

'Do please excuse me,' he told them, 'but I had to lock up the office. Speak quickly, as they're coming. How can I help you?'

'As we're all together,' said Bendu, drawing them closer to himself by their elbows, 'I want to make sure that no one but ourselves knows of the robbery.'

'You may be certain that nobody knows anything,' answered all three together, the Commissioner, the Director, and the head of the section.

'Excellent. Then you can leave the doors of the Museum wide open and let everybody go in and out as he pleases. But you must take care that not a single soul knows of this theft. All I need is an exact list, absolutely exact, of the names of all the persons who are inside at this moment, beginning with the Museum porters and ending with the French Members of Parliament. Understand me well . . . the names of each and every individual . . . even your own. And I want my name too to appear on the list. . . . Who will do this job? Hurry up, tell me, because they're coming and I must go to my place without losing any time.'

'I shall do it . . . personally,' answered the Museum Director.

'Excellent. Goodbye.' And he walked out, leaving the three of them just standing there, staring at one another.

The Maltese detective had laid his first trap with the greatest subtlety. Now nothing more was wanting but the smallest confirmation of the idea stored up in his mind, for the criminal to find himself caught in the net. For all that he had discovered up to now was by pure speculation, and he did not feel absolutely sure. A concrete proof was still needed, and he had it in mind that the solution of the precious coin robbery would probably lead to the solution of the whole series of thefts that had been going on in the best Maltese houses for over a year.

What Bendu could not understand was not who the thief was, but why that thief was stealing at all.

It is not an easy matter to understand the workings of the mind of our detective, but the foundation of every thought that passed through his mind was actual and positive. Bendu had made a careful study from every aspect of every theft that had occurred during his service with Mr. Frank Gatt. He had now amassed plenty of data, and nothing was left but to confirm his ideas. For this reason, when he walked out of the Museum door he went up to Mr. Gatt's car, got in beside the driver, and took up again the book he had been reading before, and which he had to put aside reluctantly when the Commissioner called him.

This time, however, it was not true that he was reading!

Stretched out comfortably with the book open in his hand, Bendu was looking into the mirror in front of him, fixed to the ceiling of the car and reflecting the Museum doorway through which all the people had to pass.

Bendu Muscat was watching!

A few minutes after he had assumed that rather lazy posture, the first visitors began to appear talking among themselves in loud voices, all of them praising the beauty of our tiny Museum.

Every Maltese gentleman had a Frenchman with him, and as it was already past noon they were very probably going back to their homes, to each of which one or two of the parliamentarians had been invited.

Bendu did not take his eyes from the mirror. Bendu was watching and studying certain things that would never have occurred to anyone else.

At last the Commissioner and Madame Lucie appeared. They were accompanied by one of the highest personages, who was invited to lunch with them at Villa Hollywood.

When they were a few paces away Bendu got out from one side and the driver from the other, to open the doors of the car. Bendu arrived first, and bowed so deeply that his hand knocked against Madame Lucie's handbag, and it fell to the ground.

'Pardon, Madame,' he said as he picked it up, keeping it in his hand. Then he continued in Maltese, looking her straight in the eye, 'Shall I carry it for you, Madame Lucie?'

'No, no,' Mrs. Gatt answered quickly, and she took the bag from his hand.

They all entered the car. The Commissioner sat on the left, Madame Lucie on the right, and the French gentleman between them. Bendu and the driver took their places in front where they were before and the car moved off towards Gzira.

The Maltese detective had no need to watch any more.

Mr. Gatt's car glided as swift as an arrow towards Villa Hollywood. During the whole journey the Commissioner did not open his mouth four times altogether and then only to answer yes or no as was necessary. He was thinking of other things, things much more important: the events that had taken place a short time before in the Museum.

Mrs. Gatt, either because she was too tired after all the talking she had done during the morning visits, or because she was not feeling too well, sat even more silent than her husband.

For this reason the entire burden fell on the secretary, who had to start acting as guide once more. And as he was sitting near the driver, as we have already stated, occupying the seat opposite the Commissioner, he was obliged to sit with half his body turned back so as to be able to give the necessary information to M. Gastou—for on him had fallen Madame Lucie's choice of a guest to lunch, a figure who was known and honoured all the world over—concerning the names of the places through which they were passing, and everything worth mentioning that could be seen on the way.

In his uncomfortable position the secretary had half his back turned towards Mr. Gatt, and half his front towards M. Gastou, while his eyes were continually directed towards Mrs. Gatt. And the more he looked at her the more worried he felt.

The poor lady was surely feeling ill!

Her head drooped, both her hands were on her handbag on her lap; and every time Bendu's eyes fell on her he always found her in the same position. Whenever her husband or the guest told her anything she just lifted her eyes, answered a few words, and then lowered her head again. M. Gastou was so taken up with the guide's explanations that he observed nothing of all this.

They had not been on the road a quarter of an hour when the car pulled up opposite the Villa. The driver got out to open one of the doors; Bendu also got out to open the door on his side. The first person to come out was Mrs. Gatt, and after her their guest. On Bendu's side Mr. Gatt alighted.

They walked slowly up the steps, Madame Lucie with M. Gastou and Mr. Gatt with the secretary behind them. As they entered the hall the lady of the house invited M. Gastou into the drawing-room for a drink, and to show him her collection of portraits of film stars which in her opinion could well take their place in any museum of the world.

Seeing this, the Commissioner took the opportunity to pull Bendu aside and say to him, 'Mr. Muscat, let us go upstairs. I have something to say to you.' He then turned to M. Gastou. 'Vous permettez un moment, Monsieur Gastou, n'est-ce pas?'

'Mais oui, Monsieur le Commandant, mais oui. . . .'

The Commissioner could not wait to arrive upstairs. While he was still in the middle of the staircase he asked his secretary:

'Did you make out anything, Mr. Muscat? Do you have a clue? I see you're so calm, as if you're sure of yourself. Please don't leave me in the dark!'

'I am on the track of someone . . . .'

By now they had arrived upstairs and gone into the office. The Commissioner locked the door behind him.

'I want to make a confession, Mr. Muscat. . . .'

'Yes? . . .'

'I suspect that the guilty parties are to be found among . . . our guests. That's why I invited M. Gastou over here because . . . I suspect . . . that if he is not in it himself he may at least give us an idea, provide us with some clue.'

Muscat just stared at him, and answered briefly:

'Do you think so?'

'I don't really know, but it seems to me the whole affair was planned in advance. Whoever stole the coin was a practised hand, don't you think so?'

'Maybe,' answered the secretary drily. 'But is there anything else you wish to tell me? Because . . . I don't think it's right to leave Mr. Gastou alone. . . . We had better go downstairs. . . . Perhaps Mrs. Gatt would like to go to her room and change. . . .'

'You're right. Let's go down.'

Bendu followed him rather hurriedly, as if he were chasing someone and feared that he would escape. He went straight to the drawing-room . . . but no one was in there. He looked for them in the sitting-room; they were not there either. He went into the dining-room; the same thing! Perhaps they had gone out into the garden. He ran down the winding staircase, passed through the garage, went out of the door that led to the garden and glanced all round. He had guessed rightly. Madame Lucie and M. Gastou were at the other end of the garden, looking at the chickens on the side where the cistern stood. When he saw this he was overcome by a kind of fury. He ran up to them as if he wanted to tell them something, but . . .

What had happened? Let us go back a little.

When Mme Lucie and M. Gastou had gone into the drawing-room, and Mr. Gatt with his secretary had gone upstairs, the lady of the house had invited her guest to go down into the garden with her to see the Maltese orange-trees which, God bless them, that year were swarming with fruit. And as they arrived downstairs she asked him if he would care to look at the hen-coop where she had some lovely Leghorn hens, each finer than the other. And she was right; they were so handsome that M. Gastou was quite enchanted by them. As he gazed at them in admiration Madame Gatt walked up to the cistern and lifted the lid.

'What's in there?' asked M. Gastou as he approached her.

'This . . . this is where we collect the water for our garden. Malta isn't France. We must take care of the rain-water which God sends us.'

He had now reached her side, and he too peeped into the deep well.

'Has anything fallen out of your hand?' he asked as he lifted his head, which he had inserted into the mouth of the well to get a better view.

'No . . . nothing . . . nothing has fallen from my hand. . . .'

'Something has certainly fallen into the well. . . . Look . . . the water is still moving.'

'No . . . no . . .,' Madame Gatt repeated. 'Perhaps a small stone fell in from the edge. . . .'

'Maybe. . . .'

A moment before Bendu had arrived beside them and had overheard the last words. So he too looked into the well with great attention. When he saw the ripples that appear on the surface when some object is thrown into water, he bit his lower lip so hard that the blood came.

Bendu had arrived just one moment too late!

I. MUSCAT-AŻŻOPARDI

A House upon Sand

A COMEDY IN ONE ACT

Time: Always or never in Malta

DRAMATIS PERSONAE

LELI *Husband of*
PAWLA *Mother of*
MARY *and* JOHNNY
NERIKU Pawla's father
WENZA Pawla's niece
Police Sergeant
Two Labourers

THE scene reveals a common room with old plaster on the walls. It is Pawla's house. There is now some new furniture in the room which gives it a better appearance. There appears a sofa and some arm-chairs, chairs scattered here and there, and a mahogany table; facing the audience is a cocktail cabinet, and a couple of fine pictures lie on the table waiting to be hung. A door in the middle of the stage is the main entrance of the house, and another to the left of the actors leads to the other rooms. A huge wireless set is playing loudly as the curtain rises.

(PAWLA, *more or less well-dressed, looks towards the main entrance through which two labourers are carrying an arm-chair. As soon as she sees them she shuts off the wireless.*)

PAWLA: Come in, come in friends. Don't worry about the wall, we'll be plastering that inside and out, or perhaps we'll paint it. Paint is better.

(*The two men come in with the last piece of furniture, an arm-chair belonging to the set.*)

FIRST MAN: That's the lot, ma'm, ain't it?

PAWLA: Yes, you've brought in the whole set. Everything's in order.

SECOND MAN: Then we're off now, ma'm.

PAWLA: Just a minute. (*She goes inside to fetch a couple of pound notes, comes out and gives them one each.*) There's one for each of you. Share and share alike.

FIRST MAN: Thank you very much, ma'm. If only everyone was like you. Good-day.

PAWLA: Good-day, my man. Tell your boss that we'll call tomorrow to pay him. (*The men go out.*) What lovely furniture! Just look at the sofa! At long last I've got my wish. (*She goes to the armchair, and like a child bumps up and down on the springs.*)

MARY (*entering in evening dress*): See how it fits me, Ma. Sweet, isn't it? Does it suit me, Ma?

PAWLA: How awful that Ma sounds. It's Mama now, not Ma. I've told you how many times, not Ma.

MARY: Anyway, what do you think of it, Mama? (*with emphasis.*)

PAWLA (*looking at it closely*): What do *I* think of it? I've never been to any balls. I've never worn any evening dress, and I don't understand much about them; but it looks very nice.

MARY: I thought so too, from what I could see. Look here, we need a long mirror. The one we've got is too small.

PAWLA: All right, we'll buy one. But do you know what you ought to do? Take the dress to the dress-maker and see what she says. She would under-stand. (*After a pause*) Mary, have you seen the drawing-room set?

MARY: Oh, I'm out of my mind! How lovely! Simply beautiful! Now all we need is a good coat of plaster, Ma.

PAWLA: Plaster? Paint all over, unless we rent a house in Sliema and leave here.

MARY: Oh yes, that's the place to go to; I'm fed up with this place too. The neighbours always have their eyes on us, they like to mind everybody else's business.

PAWLA: That's true for sure. When we were poor and without a penny everybody used to say 'Poor Pawla!' Now that we're well off they'd all like to shoot at us—with the gun of a warship!

MARY: That's a fact. You've just reminded me. Yesterday when I was coming back from midday Mass I overheard the daughter of the family oppo-site us, the eldest one, saying to her sister, 'H'm! Fur coats now in the early morning for Mass! How grand we've become! Where does it all come from? Some good fairy must be looking after them.'

PAWLA: Let them whisper. Now I shall buy a car to spite them, just to break their hearts properly. A posh car, a seven-seater.

MARY: Even Willie my boy-friend said that his sister said to him, 'Who do you think you're marrying? A couple of days ago she was nothing but a house-maid and her brother was a bus-conductor, and her father had patches on his trousers. Now they're playing the grand,' she said.

PAWLA: But now your father's *Mister* Manwel, tell Willie's sister *that*, and you're *Miss* Mary. That's how Willie should answer his sister.

MARY: That's right, that's what I'll tell him. Well now, did you like the dress?

PAWLA: *I* liked it, though I don't understand much about it, darling. But please God the time will come when I shall understand.

MARY: It will be rather funny at the ball tonight. Dressed up fine in evening dress, and I can't dance.

PAWLA: Oh, Willie will spin you round and you'll get on all right; you're a woman and that's enough, my child. Besides, your brother can dance, he'll teach you a couple of steps too. Now it's me who's going to learn to dance; that'll make the neighbours more jealous than ever.

MARY: As if Dad will let you. . . .

PAWLA: Mary, not Dad. Papa.

MARY: I always forget. But who knows if Papa will let you?

PAWLA: He'll have to, because now I want to get on in society.

JOHN (*coming in, well-dressed, with a flashy tie*): Ma, I've just called at the tailor's for my suit. I told him, 'If it's not ready by this evening you can jolly well keep it, because I won't take it and it can jolly well stay here.' He was terrified. He said, 'You may be sure that it will be ready, sir.' I said, 'That's enough. I want to wear it for the ball.'

PAWLA: It must be a long time since you were there,

because he's brought it and hung it inside on the
back of a chair.

JOHN: It's a good thing he has, because if I pay out
my money I want to be well served.

MARY: Johnny, after we've eaten teach me a couple of
dance-steps. I want to dance with Willie tonight.

JOHN: Oh, dancing's so easy, everything's as plain
as plain. You'll soon learn.

PAWLA: It wasn't like that when I was a girl. Everything was so difficult, what with counter-steps,
mazurkas. . . .

JOHN: Look, Mary, for instance. In the Samba you
raise your leg with the beat (*demonstrating*). Well,
I'll show you later, when we've eaten.

PAWLA: How sweet! Just imagine what we've been
missing all this time. Who'd have ever believed,
Mary, that you'd be going to a high-class ball.

JOHN (*noticing the furniture*): Congratulations, Ma,
what lovely furniture. So they did bring it.

PAWLA: It's pretty, isn't it?

JOHN: Very. Now I'll go and hang my clothes in the
wardrobe.

MARY: And I'm going to slip mine off and take it to
the dressmaker to get her opinion.

PAWLA: Careful how you wrap it up, Mary. Do it
gently, mind.

MARY: You bet!

JOHN (*to his sister as they go out*): I've ordered a taxi
for this evening. It'll come for us at the door at
seven. (*They walk out talking together.*)

PAWLA (*goes out after them, comes in again with a
flower vase, places it on the cocktail cabinet but is not*

satisfied with it. She goes out again and returns with another): Oh no, how ugly! How old-fashioned! (*She puts things in their proper place again, takes up the pictures one after the other and nods approvingly.*)

LELI (*a man of about fifty, rather pale, wearing a black suit and a muffler*): I just can't pop my head out for an instant without being pestered with requests. One wants a contribution for the fireworks, another for the new banner; everyone wants something. It was much better before when no one knew me.

PAWLA: Well, you must expect that now. But don't be a miser, be generous; bit by bit you'll come to be known as a benefactor.

LELI: I've nothing to say against that; but too much is waste, Pawla.

PAWLA: Look around, Leli. What do you think of the drawing-room furniture? They've just brought it; make sure you call and pay for it tomorrow.

LELI (*gladly*): Of course I will. It's really fine. The room looks quite different now from when Cikku the grocer put in the bailiffs.

PAWLA: You wait, he'll be paid back. But don't say the word bailiffs any more. Don't remind me of the time when we had just floor and ceiling. How dreadful that was. Now we must think only of the present. Forget the past, Leli.

LELI: True enough, things were pretty bad for us in the past. The present's more pleasant. So we'll think of the present.

PAWLA: Was it for your usual ten o'clock cup you came in, Leli?

LELI: No. I left my wallet on the dressing-table and came to fetch it. I have a mania for forgetting it.

PAWLA: Nobody's going to touch it. I put it in the drawer of the bedside cupboard.

LELI (*goes in to fetch the wallet and enters again*): I'm off. If anyone asks for me, I'm at the Chemist's.

PAWLA: Won't you have a cup of tea?

LELI: No, it'll soon be lunch time. I'm off.

PAWLA: Then take a drop of brandy.

LELI: Not me, I've just taken my heart-drops. Do you want to kill me?

PAWLA: You know what I'm thinking? Who'd have thought a short time ago that Sur Tumas would have received you into his dispensary?

LELI (*smiling, reminding her of what she said before*): Forget all about the past, Pawla. (*Fondling her*) Now we must think only of the present. (*Exit.*)

PAWLA (*calling*): Mary, Mary!

MARY (*after a short while enters with a bundle in her hand*): What do you want, Mama? I was just going to the dressmaker.

PAWLA: What colour do you think is best for the drawing-room curtains? Red? Green?

MARY: I don't understand much about colours, but the lady I was last working for used to match them with the drawing-room. What do you think of that?

PAWLA: Yes. Tomorrow we'll go in to town together and buy them, whatever price they ask, because it's too bare without curtains. Yes, we'll go to the Chinese shop.

MARY: Fine, that's what we'll do tomorrow. Now I'm off to the dressmaker to get her opinion.

PAWLA: Go along then, and don't be long.

MARY: It's not far. I'll be back in a minute. I'm off, Ma. Bless me. I kiss your hand.

PAWLA: Let her have a good look at it.

MARY: Bless you. (*Exit.*)

JOHN (*enters from the adjoining room*): I'm off to the club to play a game of billiards.

PAWLA: You're always at the club, John. Why don't you go for a walk in the fresh air? You're always shut in.

JOHN: Let me alone. They've made me treasurer now.

PAWLA: Really? (*Smiling*) Congratulations! Treasurer?

JOHN: That's right. So now it's 'Sur Johnny' here and 'Sur Johnny' there.

PAWLA: Eh, but the title Sur Johnny suits you fine.

JOHN: I'm off.

PAWLA: Does the new suit fit you?

JOHN: I'll try it on when I come back. I think it'll do. (*Exit.*)

NERIKU (*enters with no jacket on, with rubber shoes, wearing a cap, a patched pair of trousers, and a torn shirt—cheap but clean—calling as he comes in*): Pawla, Pawla!

PAWLA: Yes, Pa?

NERIKU: I've come to have a word with you. (*Has a good look round and sits down.*)

PAWLA (*grudgingly*): Yes, Pa? What do you want?

NERIKU (*lighting a cigarette*): I've just been to get my old age pension, mate. Me. All that walk just for twelve bob—hardly enough to buy bread for your mother and me.

PAWLA: Really?

NERIKU: Really, my girl. I should be ashamed of myself, or rather my children should be ashamed that they're not able to fork out twelve bob between them and let me go for this silly sum, along with all those other old chaps, as if I was starving.

PAWLA: Why, Pa, you're only doing what other people do.

NERIKU (*not listening*): If you could collect something among yourselves I wouldn't need to take the twelve shillings from the Government, perhaps someone else might draw them who's in greater need than me. True, your brothers and sisters are all cluttered up with children and their pay's small . . . .

PAWLA: Look here, Pa, I've had enough of your sarcastic remarks this morning. And when you come here dress yourself well, d'you understand? Think of people seeing you coming in so shabby, without a jacket.

NERIKU: Have you got an old jacket of Leli's?

PAWLA: If I find one I'll send it over.

NERIKU: You see, my girl. The Lord knows how much money I made during the other war, and now here I am fetching my old age pension.

PAWLA: Don't forget there were eleven of us, Pa.

NERIKU: Yes, but don't you forget that it was me who earned the money, and today I don't have two farthings to rub together. (*He throws away his cigarette end. Pawla picks it up.*)

PAWLA: Well, you get twelve bob, Ma gets another twelve, and you do odd jobs. You shouldn't manage so badly.

NERIKU (*rising*): But how do some people do it? (*Looking round*) I was careful enough with my money. Now take your Leli . . . .

PAWLA: You're always harping on the same subject. You're always carrying on about my Leli.

NERIKU: That's because I'm really staggered. One day he's a painter, living from hand to mouth, and the next he's Sur Manwel. Even though he is your husband, my daughter's husband, one can't help wondering. How? Where from?

PAWLA: That's his business, Pa. He does the fiddling: his duty is to bring home what he earns. Come, would you like a drop of whisky?

NERIKU: Never mind your drop of whisky. Look here, my child, I'm your father, and it's my duty . . . .

PAWLA (*to cut him short*): Would you like a cup of tea, or coffee?

NERIKU: No, I'm going away if you're not prepared to answer. Your mother too, she thinks the same as me. She very often talks to me about it. But where are the children?

PAWLA: They've gone out. Johnny is at the club and Mary's at the dressmaker's.

NERIKU (*sarcastically*): So Marija's gone to the dressmaker's. Bless them for me, Pawla.

PAWLA: What, are you going? Won't you have anything?

NERIKU: Be blessed from earth to heaven!

PAWLA: Yes, do bless me, Pa. Give my love to Ma.

NERIKU: I'll give your love to your mother. I'm off.

(*Goes out. Pawla goes to the door and gazes after him. Then she walks back with bowed head.*)

PAWLA: How? Where from?

WENZA (*outside*): Aunt! Aunty! . . . Aunt Pawla! . . .

PAWLA (*stops with a fright*): What's up with her at this time of the day? (*Shows that she is not pleased with the visit*) Come in.

WENZA (*walks in with a baby in her arms, her hair dishevelled*): Good morning Aunty. Grandpa has just been here, hasn't he?

PAWLA (*drily*): Good-day. Yes.

WENZA (*looking round*): Oh, what lovely furniture. Have you just bought all this, Aunt Pawla?

PAWLA: Yes.

WENZA: I thought as much, because the last time I came it wasn't here.

PAWLA: Well, it's here now, Wenz.

WENZA: Eh! Them that have pepper should spray it on the cole-wort.

PAWLA: When we had no pepper no one used to spray it on us, Wenz.

WENZA: I think of you. I think of you plenty.

PAWLA: Indeed. (*Changing the subject*) Shall I make you a cup of tea? You've come in at a bad time. I'm in such a muddle. Will you have a cup of tea?

WENZA: No thanks, I've just had one at my mother's.

PAWLA: You're to blame if I'm inhospitable.

WENZA (*sitting down*): Great misery's fallen on the island, and there's worse to come.

PAWLA (*tidying up still*): Really? Well, that's only to be expected after such a war.

WENZA: It's said there are going to be more sackings.

PAWLA: Ooh! Do talk about something else, Wenz. What gloomy talk, sackings and misery! Change the subject.

WENZA: All the same my Salvu hasn't found a job yet, and it's almost six months now. Imagine what that means, six months with nothing coming in, not a farthing.

PAWLA: Why doesn't he emigrate, go to Australia?

WENZA: And where will the passage-money come from?

PAWLA: The Government will give him something.

WENZA: Ha! We'd have fared badly if it hadn't been for my mother, God bless her. But poor darling, how long can she support us?

PAWLA: Yes, but your mother is always your mother, and it's her you must fall back on, for she is your mother.

WENZA: That's quite right, one must fall back on one's mother. But my mother's not a millionaire.

PAWLA: Yes, but . . . . It's only on her you have a claim.

WENZA: But poor dear, one must be prudent, too.

PAWLA: Now suppose, God forbid, my daughter Mary gets married and falls in need, would I deny her?

WENZA: If my mother had as much money as you for instance . . . .

PAWLA: Ah! Is that what all these hints are in aid of? I've got your meaning, Wenza. Now look here. What we have's our own, and we got it by the sweat of our brow, so if you're thinking . . .

WENZA: By the sweat . . . (*laughing*).

PAWLA: What are you laughing for? By my husband's, your uncle's sweat. And we've no intention of distributing it to other people.

WENZA: I was simply going to tell you . . .

PAWLA: What?

WENZA: That my little girl has had scarlet fever, and what with the doctor's fees, and Salvu being out of work. . . . What I wanted to say was, couldn't you let me have at least five pounds?

PAWLA: There we are. Only yesterday my sister Katarin came and wanted me to lend her twenty pounds. I'd better not say anything. Once get started, and if we go on encouraging everyone who comes to beg from us we'll end up where we were before, and even worse off.

WENZA: And didn't you get by all right?

PAWLA: Just like now, you bet!

WENZA: There must be charity, Aunty, even towards strangers; how much more with your own folk? Aunt Katarin helped you so much when you were in need (*getting angry*).

PAWLA: Now look here, have you come here to make me trouble?

WENZA: I came for the five pounds, but now I don't want them at all. Have you already forgotten how you came crying to my mother when they cleared you out from floor to ceiling?

PAWLA: Go away, Wenza, go away. It's much better.

WENZA: So now you're turning me out? Now you don't want us to talk to you, because you've become rich? Without anyone knowing how. And how?

Where from? Everybody's wondering about you,
where the money came from.

PAWLA: Let them wonder, Wenz. My husband knows
the how and the wherefrom. It's no one else's business.

WENZA: Money doesn't come from nothing, Aunty.

PAWLA: Go out please, Wenza, and be careful what
you say. Are you leaving, or must I push you out?

WENZA: All right, I'm going . . . I'm not going to
carry away any of the spring armchairs you've just
bought.

PAWLA: Go. It's better for both me and you.

WENZA: Good-bye, Aunty. (*Exit.*)

PAWLA (*looking after Wenza*): Jealousy! (*She turns
round into the room in a thoughtful mood.*) How?
Where from? After all, it's true. How? Where from?
(*Remains thoughtful.*)

LELI (*enters with his hands in his pockets*): Near the
chemist's I saw some stone-cutters eating such huge
hunks of bread and oil that they've whetted my
appetite. I've come to raid the larder. (*About to go
into the next room.*)

PAWLA (*stopping him*): Leli, listen!

LELI: What is it, Pawla? By the way, I saw your
father a short time back. Has he been in?

PAWLA: Never mind about my father. He's an *honest*
man.

LELI: Who said he wasn't? Who's offended him?
(*Going out again.*)

PAWLA: Look here, every time I ask you a question
you always avoid giving me a straight answer.
I've always been faithful to you and never pestered

you with questions. I believed in you. I've never had the least doubt or suspicion about you. But today I want you to answer me. You must.

LELI (*laughing*): The usual questions! Let the world go on its own sweet way.

PAWLA: Don't laugh. Where is all this money coming from? Today I want a definite answer, not the usual 'Shut up', or no answer at all, or 'Cut it short'. Today I want to know, and seriously. How? Where from? Come on, answer me.

LELI: Pawla dear, aren't you living like a lady? So what business is it of yours? You get all you want and go short of nothing.

PAWLA: What business is it of mine? Aren't I your wife? It's me that gets all the nasty remarks from people, even from the family.

LELI: Just let them talk. It's all envy.

PAWLA: But shouldn't *I* know?

LELI: Better not. Look, I reason it out this way; however the money comes, if you know about it, a woman—don't be offended, Pawla—it'll do much harm.

PAWLA: Much harm? Much harm? Then the money's not coming the right way, as God wants it? It must be so if it's harmful for me to know about it.

LELI: You *are* getting worked up today, Pawla! The money I give you, haven't you always paid for things with it? Haven't you always made good use of it? Eh? Understand?

PAWLA: No, I don't understand. But today I want to understand. I just must understand. My niece Wenza and my father today confirmed my suspicions. What are you going to do? What will you tell me?

LELI: I'm afraid you'll let slip some word and . . .

PAWLA: Well, what will happen if I do let some word slip?

LELI: You'll let the cat out of the bag.

PAWLA: Let the cat out of the bag? My God, then what's going on behind my back?

LELI: Let's cut it short; it's better—we've always done so. And don't shout, don't shout . . .

PAWLA: Leli (*looks at him threateningly*), how is this money coming in? Speak! (*Pause.*) Hurry up, speak, Leli. (*Another pause.*)

LELI: Where are the children?

PAWLA: They've gone out. We're all alone. You can speak.

LELI (*looking around*): I'm forging money.

PAWLA: Forging money? Then people were right after all, my mother and father, and Wenza. Aren't you ashamed of yourself? This very day you can take everything back, I want nothing of yours. (*Throws away her wallet*) I don't want money with a curse on it, I don't want even to touch it. I'd rather go back to how I was. I was happier then. Leli, remember that sin doesn't lie snoring; you'll be caught as sure as I'm talking to you now.

LELI (*in an affected voice*): Not me, I won't be caught! Why, I'm making them even better than the Mint. Really perfect.

PAWLA: I'm telling you you'll be caught, today or tomorrow, and I only hope they do catch you. But no . . . because you'll always be my husband; and then there are the children, my children. But what in the world made you do it? This is thieving!

LELI: Pawla, look out what you're saying. Let the world go hang, and don't worry me. Remember I've a weak heart. So leave me alone. Is this all the thanks I get for having made you a lady, then?

PAWLA: Leli, get out, you thief.

LELI: Thief? Why thief? Because I forge money? Who am I robbing? The Government? The Government is rich, it's got plenty of money.

PAWLA: It's robbery all the same, otherwise those who get caught wouldn't be thrown into gaol. Into gaol, do you understand?

LELI (*to himself*): Well, that's true. I'd got so used to taking risks that I'd forgotten everything about prison. You're right. (*Goes out sadly and slowly, opening the door.*) Gaol.

PAWLA (*sitting down on the sofa*): If people only knew!

MARY (*coming in, with the bundle as before*): Mama!

PAWLA (*hardly looking up*): Yes?

MARY: The bazaar near the church has some lovely curtains, at a pound a yard the man said. They are really lovely. And the evening dress just fits me. The dressmaker told me I looked like a fashion-plate. Roll on tonight and the ball!

PAWLA: Yes, daughter, yes. Go to the ball.

MARY: What's wrong, Ma? You're looking ever so upset. Are you taking after Dad and getting heart trouble?

PAWLA: Heart trouble? No. Go in, some day I'll tell you.

MARY: No, tell me now.

PAWLA: Go and get ready for the ball, and enjoy yourself . . . until . . .

MARY: Until?

PAWLA: Until . . . Oh . . . go, child.

MARY: Mum's off colour today. (*Exit.*)

PAWLA: Yes . . . Mum's off colour.

JOHN (*enthusiastically, from outside*): Ma! There's a motor-bike for sale which I'm bargaining for. I was asked fifty pounds for it. If it comes off will you give me the money?

PAWLA: Fifty pounds? (*Indifferently*) For a motor-cycle? Buy it another time.

JOHN: Do you think it too much? Only yesterday you wanted to buy us a car for £400!

PAWLA: Yes, we'll buy it all right.

JOHN: What's wrong with you, Ma?

PAWLA: Buy it another time, Johnny. Go now, my son.

JOHN (*innocently*): I'd better go. We're in a bad temper today. (*Exit.*)

SERGEANT (*knocking*): Pawla, Pawla!

PAWLA (*indifferently*): Who's there? Come in. (*The sergeant comes in.*)

SERGEANT (*coughing*): Your husband Leli . . .

PAWLA: Leli? I thought as much. I told him so. We're done for! (*Rising in a hurry*) Sergeant . . .

SERGEANT: The Inspector has sent me. We've carried Sur Manwel to the police station. Well, you know, one day or another . . .

PAWLA: One day or another he'll get caught. My words have come true. His forgery's been found out.

SERGEANT: Forgery? What are you saying?

PAWLA: My God, what have I done?

SERGEANT: I actually came in to tell you that he had a heart attack near the police station and we just took him inside. (*Reflecting*) So at last we've discovered who it is! (*Exit hurriedly.*)

PAWLA: My God, what have I done? (*Shouting*) Marija, Ġanninu! (*Mary and Johnny come in running.*)

JOHN: What's wrong, Ma?

MARY: Good gracious, Ma, what's happened?

PAWLA (*fainting*): What's happened? I built a house upon sand! The foundations have given way, it has crashed down and ground us all to powder under it. (*Mary and Johnny look at one another without understanding her. Pawla faints, and falls on the sofa.*)

CHARLES D. CLEWS

PART THREE

Poetry

G. A. BONAMICO

To Grand Master Cottoner

MAY has come with flowers and roses,
Past is lightning, cold and rain,
Earth is strewn with leaves and blossoms,
Hushed the wind, and still the main.

From the sky the clouds have vanished,
Even the uplands verdant grow,
Every bird renews its singing,
Every heart with joy does glow.

Little joy was in this Island,
Since its champion was not there;
None to guard it, it was weeping
Like a starving prisoner.

You are our delight and comfort,
Cottoner, light of our eyes,
Turning, while Heaven spares you to us,
Winter's cold to summer skies.

ANONYMOUS

Sonnet

YES, I'm in love: the truth I aye confessed:
Not since the sun began to shine on me,
Never I nourished in my inmost breast
Such love as this, engendered now by thee.

Thine eyes and mouth, my foes both worst and best,
Enslave my heart, that may not ransomed be:
Thy mouth is honey, sweetest and most blest,
Thine eyes are stars, and shine as brilliantly.

From them I learned delight and grief supreme;
The years through them as weeks to me appear;
In them I find my every hope and dream;
Endure I cannot, if they be not near;
Cheer, life and wealth mere empty words I deem;
They only are my wealth, my life, my cheer.

Ġ. MUSCAT-AZZOPARDI

Marsaxlokk

O FAIR, O tranquil night! Here, at my window,
I never weary of joying in the shine
Of the moon upon the waves that, as in a cradle,
Sway with the rocks fringing the sheltered coves.
And the trees, suddenly stirred by a soft breeze,
Silver on silver stretch their shady limbs
Towards yonder clouds of blue, where clustering stars
Glitter together, a very swarm of light.

How still! I hear an ewe calling her lambs
In the meadow the other side of the creek, and hush!
The plash of the fishermen's oars dipped in the brine.
And farther away, in the dim remote, I see
Now vanishing, now instantly flashing anew,
The coloured brightness I love on Dellimara.

St. Paul

GREAT in your self, great in your thought and zeal,
in passion and in action, even in cruelty;
if Christ's religion could have been destroyed,
you only had destroyed it in Judaea.
But God would not suffer to behold your greatness
continue ever the greatness of oppression;
He smote you unexpectedly with that flame
there, where you journeyed for the shedding of blood.

All things were changed in you, when your name was
    changed;
you became Christ's strongest arm, highest interpreter,
to Him with your heart you gave your soul and body.
Then, tossed up by the waves upon our rocks,
when, as you tell us, you escaped from drowning,
what God had wrought in you, you wrought in us.

TEMI ZAMMIT

The Old Man and Death

AN old, old man laden with firewood
Once upon a time was slowly climbing the road,
Under the weight of the load bent double,
His body worn out, numbed and weary.

He stopped, went on a few steps, staggered,
Drew a breath, stood still, panted desperately,
Till suddenly spying a heap of stones on the road
He flung himself down on them, limp and fainting.

'O death, death, only you can relieve me,'
He cried in anguish. Death immediately
Appeared before him, all compassion, to gather him
Unto herself and relieve him, the poor old man.

When he beheld that heap of bones strung together,
A scythe in her hand, her eyes deep hollows,
The old man changed his mind, began babbling with
  fear,
His knees knocking, his arms trembling.

'I know well you are compassionate,' he told her,
'So do with me the best that you are able:
Load on my shoulders this heap of firewood
And let me go on my way again home.'

Censa laughed—if Censa knows how to laugh—
And helped him up, then said to him: 'Splendid
These people are; in death's hour they forget utterly
How much they have suffered, what they have
  endured!

Go then, and live the couple of days left to you:
I wanted to deliver you out of all bondage.
Go on suffering, until on another occasion
I come on my own for you, unsummoned.'

DUN KARM

Innu Malti

Lil din l-art ħelwa, l-omm li tatna isimha,
Ħares, Mule, kif dejjem Int ħarist:
Ftakar li lilha bl-oħla dawl libbist.

Agħti, kbir Alla, id-dehen lil min jaħkimha,
Rodd il-ħniena lis-sid, saħħa 'l-ħaddiem:
Seddaq il-għaqda fil-Maltin u s-sliem.

National Anthem

KEEP watch, O Lord, as Thou has watched for ever
O'er this sweet motherland whose name we bear,
Arrayed by Thee in radiance most fair:
Grant to her rulers wisdom, just endeavour
To master-man, to worker health's increase,
Give Malta truest unity and peace.

St. John's Day

LONG centuries have passed, and your voice remains
Beautiful and strong on the day of the solemn feast,
The voice of the great Baptist echoing in the early
    dawn
Over this city, builded never to fall.
Within the church the people are gathering together
From town and countryside, and on their happy faces
I see written in light that inward joy
Which seems this day to fall upon everyone.

Your voice thunders joyfully, ponderous bell,
In the time when through the streets clean-swept and
    sunny
Passes at length the venerable Procession;
And two by two with them, over the dewy leaves
I fancy I see passing, with haughty mien
As they march onward with measured steps, the
    Knights.

Viaticum

DARKNESS profound; a cold wind whistles
Through the window cracks, and on the closed panes
The drizzling rain incessantly patters,
      And from the spouts

Water spills down the streets. On the glaze
Of the drenched ground here and there shivers
The red glow of the lamps, as if they were
      Beckoning to sleep.

Far as the eye reaches, not a soul is visible;
Anon is heard a hurrying footstep; passes
A black shape on the road, and vanishes; wheels
      Rumble afar.

Now faintly, faintly I hear the voice of a bell—
How well I have known that voice! It approaches
Growing in strength as it comes. All of a sudden
      I descry moving

Lanterns, two by two; they approach; one side
And the other of the street they divide; hasten,
In front, the children; in the midst a crimson billow
      The little banner.

Yes; they are drawing nigh. I begin to hear
The voice of the priest, and the other people; lights
Start in the windows, behind the panes, and amid
  them
      People on their knees.

Jesus is passing: in the night, the rain, the wind
Passes all pity and compassion, all love,
Going to comfort the heart and soul of a poor wretch
    In the last anguish.

Meseems there are passing with Him, hidden
From mortal gaze, multitudes of angels
Praising Him who in a piece of white bread
    All His majesty

Locked and concealed, and with holy zeal hastens
To console him who by it is fed and strengthened.
Jesus has passed: behind Him the sweet fragrance
    Of heaven lingers.

O teaching of the Faith! O holy Creed!
How beautiful you are! What heavenly wisdom!
O infinite Goodness, Thou only couldst work
    Such frenzy of love!

Ah, when for me the days of this mortal life
Draw near to their close, and sore disquieted
Under the sentence of death, I picture the past
    As all a dream,

Whether it be in the night or day, in winter
Or the fierce heat of the summer, even so, Lord,
Come visit me, with children two by two, with voices
    Praying compassion.

Last Friend, come into my bosom, and rest
Thy heart on my heart, and cleanse me of every sin:
Clinging to Thee, Jesus, I will take unafraid
    The eternal road.

Whiteness

I saw you at daybreak, laughing amid the green
Of a fragrant garden, on lily and jessamine,
Pure without spot, and over you the crimson
That bursts aflame at the birth of the kindly sun.
I saw you again in the silent noon, outstretched
On the snow, the garb and ornament of the highlands,
Shining afar upon the envious eyes
Of those who hear the quiet call of the heights.

O radiant whiteness! and in my heart was kindled
A fire of love when I saw you in the evening
Gazing pensively from the face of the moon;
And I dreamed a dream of Paradise—a new vision!—
I saw you as a veil shrouding a Jewish maiden
Who was a virgin, and held in her arms her son.

In the Catacombs

In vain will you search here for the art of beauty,
That marvellous art which once filled Athens and
   Rome
With wonders such as not ever time was able
To excel whether in power or sweetness: never
Did arrogance conceive of itself to leave
Chiselled in marble here, that of him at least
The name might remain, and he not die entirely.
Whoso descended here, having lived in the world,
Was not of the world: wealth, riches, all ornament
For him was empty and savourless. What boots it

To acquire and amass what cannot be kept for ever?
One only is Eternal, and to attain
That One who elected poverty to embrace,
All things that dazzle the eye and harden the heart
These prudent ones trampled below their feet.
Whoso descended here knew he descended
Into a sleep from which he shall rise; knew God
Shall in His might regather the dust of the tombs
Scattered hither and thither, and of that dust
Reassemble the bodies Death struck down and
    shattered.

Visit to Jesus

NEVER shall I forget the sweetness I felt
That time in my heart, O Jesus.
                        It was the season
When the vines are stripped, and to the master are
    brought
The last clusters, when with the sweet breeze
The yellow leaves go flying, and into the mist
The blue of the sky vanishes, and begins
The first freshet of rain; the time was at hand
When the birds would forgather high in the trees
And fill the air with the clamour of their voices.
I, all alone, a little weary of books,
Plunged on the road between the fields and the sea.
Sweet, sweet was your voice that day, O sea,
And quiet the wave that plashed unfoaming
Softly against the rocks. Sweet were your voices,

Trees robed eternally in your green
Who were full fashioned when a little child
I used to clutch about the knees of another
To keep myself on my feet. Toward the cottage,
His tools over his shoulder, an old countryman
Was trudging down alone, while the last singing
Of some shepherd, far distant, could be heard
With the voices and a little bell tinkling;
And over the white sea faintly appeared
The red flicker of the glistening oars
Of some fishing-smack with its impedimenta
Of nets and baskets.

              There is some connexion
Between the hour of the day and the history
Of our lives; and when the sun is just on the point
Of setting, giving its last kiss to the world,
The thoughts take wing towards the happy time
That has passed over us and is taken for ever;
There is a clutch at the heart, and involuntarily
The tears leap in our eyes, and from our soul's
Depth a sigh breaks. I thought of you, sweet time,
When I was in my father's house, and one table
Gathered us all together, in the bond of love,
Myself, my brothers, and those that begat us;
But chiefly of you, mother, who though an old woman
Of eighty years, remained to the last hour
Beautiful as you were in the best of your days,
And with the light of your eyes, that never dimmed,
You signalled to me the desires of your heart
Without ever a word spoken. I thought of you,
And seemed to sense there was nothing left for me
To love this so precious life you gave me

Now you were no more able, in joy or sorrow,
To share it with me, and under the kindly earth
I yearned to sleep, in death's embrace, with you.

The little church huddled among the trees
Stood open; I entered, and on my toes
Crept near to the altar. There was no other
Beside me at that time, and I found myself
Alone in the hush of the House of God. The red
Glow of the sun was pouring at that time
Through a little window into the church,
And on the wall opposite the lighted window
Here and there could be seen silently shaking
The shadow of the leaves obeying the sweet
Breeze of the sea. In that crimson radiance
The holy cross standing upon the altar
Was wholly shrouded. Long I gazed at the pale
Sorrowful likeness of Jesus in the redness
Of that radiance! What mighty grief I saw
In the drooping head and the unseeing eyes
Of that Silent one! Sorrow was born in my heart
For thee, the time I had wasted on vanity
Without soaring towards the heavenly good,
Though oftentimes I had felt kindled in my heart
The ardour to fly; flamed over my face
The flush of shame; again and again my gaze
Fell broken to the ground, and burning as coals
I felt the tears rolling upon my cheeks.
In that tightness of the heart my lips moved
And only these words issued: 'Our Father
Which art in heaven, hallowed be Thy name.'
If that had been the first time in my life

I heard those precious words, they would not have
    seemed
More wonderful to me than upon that night:
Never as on that day had I felt the sweetness
Of that name in my ears, never in my heart
Experienced the flaming fire of love
Fiercer or finer. I was no more alone
In that little church, seeing that now
Out of the heights of heaven reached to guard me
The mighty power of a Father who forgets not
His children ever, and in His arms receiveth
With infinite goodness all who draw nigh to Him.
'Our Father,' I called again; and I beheld
Linked in a holy bond the nations, though parted
Whether by distance or time, and the whole world
A single happy house, where alike the rulers
And they that beg on the road are brothers called.
How fair is Redemption! How near we are drawn
To life by Thy precious death, O Son of God
Crucified on the tree! Joy is not the greatest
Happiness upon earth; suffering likewise
Brings its own good, seeing that ever is found
Hidden within it the seed of deliverance:
By the weight of the cross Thou didst embrace
Our sins are lightened, and of the cruel anguish
That wrenched Thy soul from Thy body was en-
    gendered
The bond that shall not be loosed, that has bound
    securely
Under one Father all the children of earth.
Once more I repeated, 'Our Father'; and my gaze
    strayed

Over a little door on the altar, where hidden
In a shape so small, He who can do all things
Brought to nothing His majesty and power
And became our daily bread. O might unmeasured!
O frenzy of love! O goodness, goodness, goodness!
For that He willed to dwell among us and embrace
This little clay that knows only to sin,
He is infinitely compassionate. And I yearned
To love the Lord Jesus; and so poor meseemed
The common lamp that flickered there in silence
Before the Sacrament, and I longed to set
The sun in all the strength of its mighty flame
To burn before it. How lovely is the peace
Of Thy dwelling-place, O Lord! What sweet savour
Fills the house Thou hast chosen for Thy abode!
Never did arrow speed from the bow so swiftly
As swiftly sped my thoughts back to my childhood;
And I thought of the joy of that first occasion
When on my tongue, silent in mighty awe,
I savoured the taste of that pure food descending
In to my breast; of thee, sweet angel of love,
My dear mother, I thought, who soon as sprouted
Understanding in my brain, sowed in my heart the
    yearning
For that holy Bread, and perchance was the beginning
Of that other yearning which brought me to the sum-
    mit
Of the altar with Jesus. A thousand times blessed
Is the earth that received thee, and shall again restore
    thee,
In the power of that Bread, to a new life
Blissful and fair, life infinite. 'Our Father,

Our Father,' I repeated, and it seemed the sweetness
Of that most precious name left on my tongue
The savour of heaven. O never shall I forget,
Never shall I forget the sweetness I felt
That time in my heart, O Jesus.

       When I left the church
Darkness had begun to gather, and in heaven's face
Already a few stars were peeping. Alone
I returned on the road between the fields and the sea;
Again I heard upon the rocks of the shore
The wave plashing, and a sweet breeze whistling
Amid the leaves of the trees; but silent, silent
Stretched the bank; no more was to be heard
The sweet singing of the shepherd, and the country-
 man
With the voices, and the little bell tinkling.
Night was approaching, approaching; but in my
 brain
Shone a light brighter than the sun, and in my heart
Was born a new joy. Is such the speech of Heaven?
I thought no more of the past; the tears were dry
On the lids of my eyes, and like a fair star
Over my life shone forth in splendour Hope.

Non Omnis Moriar

I was half youth, half child:
 The sun of sweetest April trembled
 Above the waves of the sea—
 The sea blue as indigo, that embraces
 This island of my heart,

Red with the flowers of clover,
Green with the fields of barley:—
The scent of the orange-blossoms in the groves
Enticed me, and I took the path that winds
Between valley and field;
Sweet on my face blew
The full breeze, and in that limpid peace
I seemed to be in a dream,
A dream of light and fragrance,
A dream of love that knows no sadness.

Bewildered while I was, enchanted
  In that slumber of sweetness,
  Swift as lightning, his face the face of a star
  An angel came down from heaven—
  The Angel of Poesy—
  And with those lips, lighter than the wind that
    passes
  Cool with the setting of the sun from land to sea,
  He kissed me upon the brow
  And said to me:
  'Your portion is Singing:
  Beauty scattered over creation is your realm;
  Your happiness is of your heart and your mind.'
  I felt—I know not whether of joy or fear—
  A tremor running through my blood,
  And like a spark that kindles
  From a flint struck, kindled in my heart and
    flamed
  A longing that has not been quenched all the years
    of my life.

And I sang:
   I sang as sings beneath the sun of March
   The linnet drunk with love,
   Or else as sings in the darkness of the quiet night
   The nightingale:
   I sang as sings the water
   That limpidly leaps out of the hard rock
   And tumbles and gushes
   Until it melts in the greenness
   That knows the labour of sinewy forearms:
   I sang as sings the breeze
   Among the tops of the reeds and the trees,
   And as over some sequestered shore
   Sings, drowsy in its love, our sea.

O wonderful!
   As from my heart rose that song,
   And on the wings of words
   Soared from my mouth, like a bird from its nest,
   With a shout of joy it ran swiftly
   Not towards the tainted towns
   But in the void, betwixt the green and the blue;
   And with fine judgement it mingled
   With the melodies of the birds,
   With the fragrance of the valleys and the fields,
   With the breath of the sturdy beasts, that smoke
   White in the cool of morning,
   With the dappled hues
   Of herbs and flowers,
   And with them rose wave after wave
   Towards the clouds, beyond the clouds, beyond the
     blue.

And I thought I heard
  Out of the depths of times today forgotten,
  Out of the ruins of towns that were once
  The hearts of the world,
  Soaring silver melodies
  That sang in sweetest words
  The shape of creation and its splendour:
  Melodies of heroic men
  Who saw in the storm-tossed story of humanity
  Not the force that destroys
  But the Power that renews,
  The Power that out of the small
  Begets the great, out of the good
  The better, even as from the wheat
  Issues through death the ear: men of wisdom
  Who in the walk of life
  Cursed not the brambles of the rugged path,
  But brushed them aside and with stronger hope
  Waited, in the time of sadness,
  To peep, even afar off, the sun of peace:
  And those melodies of old
  As if drawn by some new love
  Now mingled and intertwined
  With my melody and other melodies,
  O Poesy!

Then I began to descend:
  Six and fifty winters passed over me
  And each one
  Left its track of ruin
  Within the field of my life.
  Time scored on my brow

And my cheeks lines that as the years passed
Multiplied and blackened;
My hair grizzled; the pupils of my eyes
Lost their keenness of old, and heavy
Grew the tread of my feet—
A powerful witness that the surge of blood
No more flows full within me
And clear as once it flowed
From the heart to the extremities.
My spirit is still willing; but not always
The brain answers the call of the will
And the song dies, alas, even at its birth.

And the end draws near daily.
   That hidden force
   Which pulls down and overthrows all that Life
     builds,
   And wastes and consumes that which Art yields,
   Works ever about me,
   Works, almost insensibly, and everything changes.
   When after from my eyes
   Flees the light and in black, cold darkness
   Dies the lovely vision
   Of creation that delights me
   The time may come when over the grave
   That closes over my body
   Not a tear shall fall, not a flower
   Be strewn from the hand that knows the sweetness
   Of one who loves and remembers:
   And with heart cold, forgetful
   Posterity will pass by without a single glance
   At the dwelling place of the silent poet

Yet the song shall not die:
  From under the slab
  Of the solitary grave there shall still issue clear
  The beating surge that took shape in my heart
  In the dream of my youth,
  And in a new pattern was interwoven
  With the song that I sang in the best of my days.
  An echo of the song of creation is the song
  Of the poet: of his own will
  He sings not, that enchanted one.
  As a harp sounds when trained fingers
  Run artfully over the bunched strings,
  So the poet sings
  When touched by the hand of God:
  Herald of Truth, mirror of Beauty,
  His words are from heaven, and that which in
    heaven is begotten
  Grows not old, neither dies.
  The poet perishes: the song is immortal.

A. CUSCHIERI

Christmas

How white is the moon, shining like silver!
It is as though the stars stare with amazement
at the earth's beauty, and the earth gazes
aloft entranced with thee, O light of heaven.
But hush! a tragic whisper of words wafting
from the carob-trees, there amid the fields.

    Baby, Baby at Christmas born,
    mothers for their sons do mourn.

Not so of old, countrymen, not so you sang:
  Bright stars shining in the skies
  over towns and hamlets rise;
  people from their homes emerge,
  hear the song from the vale forlorn:
  Baby, Baby at Christmas born.

Upon the day of Thy birth, great God, I desired
to banish from my heart all thought of these times
and to let my voice be heard rejoicing about Thee,
praising Thee in the peace where Thou art King;
but the words issued with tears from my mouth,
issued clothed in the sorrow of the spirit,
sorrow, because the nations see themselves tossed
in a sea of blood, drowning, scarce holding out.

  Baby, Baby at Christmas born,
  mothers for their sons do mourn.

Out of a white cloud shining as if of silver
what do you gaze on, moon, like one distraught?
Yes, you have seen truly: not water, not water;
that is the blood of brothers, rivers of tears.

  Child Jesus, who to
  redeem us, this morn
  all in a manger
  on straw wert born
  proclaim from heaven
  Thy holy call
  shall never fail us:
  Thou art over all.

What foolish wisdom was that, before Christ's birth?
One weeps to think of it! Goes he not to the grave,
every creature born? Does not death ever walk
behind us, like a shepherd behind his flock,
driving us to the dust that shall cover us?
Time destroys everything. A fool is he
who stores up wealth; you are a fool, over books
summer and winter, night and day, all the time
pondering there alone. Now tell me, truth—
what is it? where? From whom comes it? What do you
    know
of the world? What do you know of your own self?
Whence came the sun? This earth, whence does it
    come?
How do the herbs grow? How do they live and die?
Who taught the birds to build their nests, and how?
How and who taught the fishes all that they know?
And you—what are you? What is this heart, that
    surges
ever like a bottomless ocean? A child chasing
a butterfly is the learned; and he who expects
and fondly hopes for renown after his death
is as one who would catch in his hands a shadow.
Think for today only; the future is as the past;
what has been has been, and will never return.
So out with the wine you are blest with, wise man
in truth; summon around your table laden
with all good things lads and lasses; eat and drink
to purge from your head every thought of sadness;
then seize to you out of the women about you,
to the clapping of your companions, the one most
    lovely

and dance with her, dance with her; what comes after
you know only too well.—That, before Christ,
was the world's wisdom; even so our forefathers
thought, till the time that in Bethlehem's cave was
  born
Love. Pitiful wisdom, that sought again to raise
your head from the grave, go you this day before
Him who is born, and seek pardon for the wrong
you have wrought. He only is the Wisdom of life!

     Baby, Baby at Christmas born . . .
Sing on, good countryman. Not for ever the whirlwinds
will toss and twist and pluck from its roots the oak,
not ever shall black clouds scud over our heads,
not for ever shall the ocean chastise the shores.

     Wherefore God
     born this happy day
     come, adore
     yeomen blithe and gay;

     to deliver our hearts
     out of care
     He is born of a Virgin
     so fair.
     Even now
     in the cave showing
     her sweet face
     as with fire is glowing.
     Unto Him, yeomen,

be you sped
and He will lay His hands
on your head,
the poor among you to bless
and comfort those in distress.

The bells of the village are ringing,
the old men to church are all gone,
the married are there with their children,
at home remains not anyone.

In the pulpit the child is ascending
to recall the abounding joy,
to recall the shout of the prophets
foretelling the birth of a Boy.

The gate of heaven is opened
whence the sun rises, and over the world's shadows
shines forth, even as our fathers so much yearned,
the sun of truth. Flee away,
you cruel foemen: to us
at last is come, and shall never leave us
the Power that redeems us,
that banishes from us
the sorrow and bitterness of the first sin;
bondage shall be ended once and for ever,
sin's chains shall be broken,
over this earth of violence, Righteousness
and Truth once again meet, and kiss each other.

Rejoice, you prophets,
in the birth of the Child—the Son

you proclaimed now is given;
within the cave, upon straw
He is born of a Virgin, the stock
of David, the desire of all times, the hope
and glory of Sion. Rejoice,
O Bethlehem, not the least
among the cities of Judah;
their names shall perish
but not thine; thou shalt remain
forever renowned among all nations.
Rejoice, palm-tree of Kadesh,
you, Tabor and Carmel, and you other mountains
here in the Holy Land, rejoice!
Rejoice ye, earth, sky and sea:
today is born the Saviour of the World.

But thy praise above all, Mary,
the childish tongue doth raise,
praying thee to enter into us,
and so every villager prays.

Mother of sweetness past compare,
Mother of the sad heart that sighs,
upon this prayer of the villagers
let fall thy pitying eyes,
let fall on us, Mary, and see
the pains of all humanity.

Thou dost send the rain upon us
when unto thee we honour pay,
thou givest unto our seeds increase
forthwith, as unto thee we pray:

thou, who art able all to do,
suffer no more this blood to flow.

Mary, do not tell the God-child
cradled by thee, now at peace
there in Bethlehem, in the manger,
thou wilt make our grief to cease:
for the sins we wrought, we know
we deserve far greater woe.

Yet thou art kind, compassionate:
dry our mothers' tear-stained eyes;
be thyself our consolation,
chosen Mother of the skies,
that our village lives may bear
joy and sweetness past compare.

The Maltese Language

BUT this, friend of my heart,
I have; this God gave me,
this word in whose beauty
you see me now delighting.

Who said that it is heavy, and crawls
like a snake creeping on its belly?
See, how light it is,
how suddenly it leaps and soars;

It soars, and out of the mid-sky
she who was reared in the sun
glides in the loveliest blue,
looks down to earth, and again

Descends; you know not if white
it be, or yellow, or blue;
you only glimpse it changing,
becoming small as a bee

And entering into gardens,
passing among the leaves,
creeping into every blossom,
sucking the juice of the flowers.

Then it comes along sweetly
to set it upon my tongue,
buzzes loud in my ear
and makes me great and happy.

But this, friend of my heart,
I have; this God gave me,
this word in whose beauty
you see me now delighting.

As in his forge the smith
first of all heats the iron,
then little by little works it
till it takes the shape he desires,

Till it takes the shape and form
of a leaf somewhat languid
as if the sun had burned it
or the wind passed over it;

So from my hand the word
I let not go carelessly,
like one who hurls a stone
not knowing where it will fall;

But before, I soften it
in my mind like to a paste,
then slowly and patiently
I give it shape and beauty.

And I go on staring at it
to see if it sits right,
whether it slumbers or is paralysed
or if it lacks some sweetness:

And when alive and stirring
I see it pleases my friends,
then (why should I be shy to say it?)
I take delight in my thought

And in the word that rises
from my heart to my mouth
pure, sweet and beautiful
even as my mother taught me,

As once in Valletta, as you still
today hear it in the villages
without trappings on its breast,
poor, but possessing all.

But this, friend of my heart,
I have; this God gave me,
this word in whose beauty
you see me now delighting.

See how lovely it is
like a bunch of May flowers:
not sweeter is the fragrance
of basil and pennyroyal.

Not so pure is the dew
that falls upon the leaves:
it possesses the moonlight,
it possesses the lightning.

Now like one who is afraid
it steals slowly, slowly,
now it darts forth swiftly
like a bird from its nest;

Now it makes you to hear
a song of new sweetness,
then it breaks into weeping
and you hear as if a sigh;

You hear as when the sea
begins lapping our shore,
as when the wind in winter
whistles through the boughs.

A. CREMONA

The Sentinel

DARKNESS falls, and a silence reigns.
On the tongue of jutting rocks
in the mouth of Gzira Creek

an inquisitive moon discloses
demolished houses
here and there by the shores and uplands
blotted with frightening shadows
amidst a sea calm as a pool,
and on the edge of the wasteland
their heads raised high
over the rooftops and the garden
the barracks and the fortress.
All is extinct: the lights which formerly
used to shine from a hundred windows
on that eminence
every night
how they are hidden from the eye that yearns for
even a thread of the light of peace,
all in silence, all in blackness
as though they sensed envy engendered
in the stars of the heavens.

Midnight has struck. The moon
seems this while to have rested her still
gaze on these rocks,
and only converses with her
the little wave
murmuring around the beach
as if it senses the menace
of some coming disaster.
From the far horizon emerges
wandering about the heavens
a beam of light, stalking.
And still the silence reigns.

And you only hear, passing
along the gateway of the fortress,
the sentry stamping his feet.

In the empty streets, from the houses you fancy
you hear, with the breathing of people half asleep
   there,
the beat of their hearts.
There beside a little boy
stretched under a window, Fido the dog waits
to be wakened by the warning wail of disaster
and of death over this island.
At watch on the enemy he dreams, contented
with his nightly duty,
only half asleep like the others in this street,
and his heart goes pit-a-pat.
See, see how he keeps his ears pricked:
with his eyes half-closed
as though he is listening . . .
and his mind is gathering a black
cloud of foreboding.

Above the rocks beneath the walls of the fortress
that Manoel built between Ta' Xbiex and Gzira,
where now the cannon lifts up its mouth of
murderous fire, can be heard the siren.
The dog raises his head, hoists himself
on his forepaws, and stays again listening. . . .
When after a little the silence of the
night is shattered by the wailing note
announcing the enemy,

Fido, as when a greyhound slips from
the leash of its master,
leaps up, wags his tail, and starts barking
all around the little boy to waken him,
lifting up his head and calling his master
and all the people in the house, a warning shout
that the foe approaches.
And still he barks, barks unceasingly
till he hears footsteps, and the door is flung open.
A flash of lightning
is not so swift as his racing
out into the street.—Never so handsome,
joyful, alert, eyes flashing with the fire
in his heart which beats in time with his wagging tail,
with his legs leaping, with his head shaking,
never so handsome as at that moment
Fido appeared.
None so glad as Fido that slumber is scattered,
that his thoughts and desires are no more sleeping.

Still through the heavens
dragged out the last groan of that outcry
announcing the enemy approaching
towards these shores.
Still some folk had scarcely opened their eyes
and the silence of the night
still reigned, broken only by the faint sound
of some door closing,
of some footsteps hurrying
towards some hole of a shelter,
when Fido, impatient, with tireless panting
like a horse flinging the steam from its nostrils

and the fire from its hoofs
in a mad gallop,
made the rounds of all the streets along the shore
running and barking, still untiring,
not leaving any street or house
asleep behind him.
And he only stops when to his warning
responds not a sound in street or house;
he stops, and barks as if to shake
some loiterer from his slumber.
And the moon with her still eyes halts with him
watching and waiting
as upon Fido's running that night
the lives of certain folk depended.

In the rock-hollow were taking cover
from the fiery fury of the airborne enemy
children, young folk, elderly,
sleepy, worn-out;
some shivering with cold and terror,
faces cast down,
some crouched in a corner, night and day idle,
others with pale countenance
in their eyes the sunset
of the hateful time of today
flickering with its last spark.
Also in that hewn-out cavern
Fido is found by the side of his
little master lying, eyes half-open;
he twists and turns, his sleep scattered
as when a fly
he chases away from him,

while in that silence,
broken by the drone of an aircraft
approaching from afar,
nothing is heard but a whisper and a sigh or two
of people with weary lips.
A growl of thunder in the distance, then a noise
like rumbling cartwheels in the dark sky
approaching, always approaching
over housetops, ramparts, churches,
striking silent all whose lips were moving;
and nothing is heard but their hearts beating,
and their blood freezes, they crouch on the floor of
    their cavern
looking at one another, succouring one another
with trembling of the lips.
Then came the sound of an iron door slamming
after the howl of a wind, after a whistling
that shook the flame of the candle
which barely broke the frightening darkness:
an explosion of a bomb directly overhead
shook beneath their feet
the rocks of their shelter,
and their hearts sensed the first faintness of death.

As though he could find neither patience
nor repose, Fido raised his head
and stood on his fore-paws, listening
with anxious eyes.
Tongues of fire from the ground, a mighty explosion
from here and there
through the four quarters of the island:
lights racing through the skies, stars prying,

the drone of a hundred wheels
growing distant in the air . . .
the mind dreams in that instant of terror
that seems never to pass;
when with the dawn suddenly there fell
a pall of silence,
then out of the red horizon
shrilled the full-bodied blast
all of cheer
announcing the enemy had gone. . . .
Fido leaps up gladly, wagging his tail,
barking and leaping
about the legs of his little master
who, wrapped up in a blanket, with the throng
from the shelter
comes forth from that cavern
with a face of suffering,
with half-closed eyes
towards the horizon, whence the hideous clouds
of a rain all poison
still rises above this land,
with a face of torture,
with misty eyes
towards the light of a dawn clouded in blood.

It was the morn of a dawn suffused in blood
when, stretched out under a wall in the tepid sun
of autumn, dozing after a long
vigil, lay Fido,
and his little master, just away from him
his face beaming with the radiance
of innocent joy,

without a thought of the horror
of the times, the greed and deceit of wicked men,
with a heart pure of every allurement
attached to none but the heart of Fido,
was playing with his friends; when like an arrow
rushing down the road came
a lorry with engine roaring frighteningly
just as the child, utterly absorbed in
play, chasing his playmates, ran across
the street, his eyes closed.
Suddenly was heard the wail of the siren
announcing the approach of the airborne enemy,
and Fido moved at once, his slumber
scattered, raised his head
and perceived his little master in the path
of the lorry, threatened by
death, and pictured him already
crushed under the wheels. . . .
He gets up, pauses, then makes a leap,
throwing himself on the little boy,
barking and springing up at him
as quick as a lightning-flash.
The child is dragged to the ground,
pulled clear of the wheels,
snatched from the very jaws of death;
but poor Fido,
as if snatched
in the greedy claws of some ravenous ogre,
his luck evil, was swallowed up,
destroyed instantly. His pitiful howl,
the last cry that issued from Fido's breast,
stabbed the hearts of all on that beach.

Fido's death was the heaviest burden
of grief and tears.
Every night the people weep for him
when with weary eyes
their hearts go pit-a-pat, waiting to be aroused
by the loving bark of their friend Fido;
the empty houses weep for him, the houses demo-
    lished
on the jutting rocks
in the mouth of Gzira Creek.
Even the siren
with her long wail weeps for him
when at night she hears the enemy approaching
and vainly howls and howls
waiting for Fido's voice to answer her,
her nightly companion;
of Fido only the memory remains.
Everyone is sunk in slumber profound;
the moon alone is awake, with eyes staring
upon the heap of rubble
covering the bones of the sentinel of the beach,
watching still, dumbly
while on the horizon the lightning flashes.

The Sorceress

I DREAMED of you, old woman's face
with your mouth
with two teeth grinning,
the hollows of your eyes
two smouldering flames
billowing smoke and stench in a cloud of fear.

I dreamed of you, old woman's face
with two fingers
wrinkled, and long, sharp nails
of a cruel falcon
picking at bones and sniffing
the odour of blood—

the bones of nice fat children
shut in a cage
of iron—of children stolen
by the demon
they frighten children with, because he drinks our
  blood!

With goggling eyes we heard
from the mouth
of the old woman the story of you, sorceress,
and in our childhood
we were used to your living likeness in our brain.

I saw you in a dark room
by the flickering
light of a lantern and amid the howl
of the screeching wind
reading palms, snapping and heartening hope.

I saw you limned in the brain
of the most powerful
minds of writers
opening the door
of the unseen,
billed as the wisest and most loathsome of hags!

Deep in the cave, in the shadows
with a face
lit up by flames,
dissolving in a cauldron
the heads and tongues
of people forgotten by the vanity of this life.

But also in that cauldron
all poison dissolving
with the tongues of many serpents, there was
the blood
of her that I loved—and her heart and her head.

MARY MEYLAQ

On a Rainy Day

TODAY the ceiling is leaden,
Now and again a snake of fire,
A flash of lightning, thunder—
What can you expect of January?

Oh! Oh! look what's coming from the south-west
And how dark it's getting, good heavens!
The sky has closed its eyes,
We'll surely be drenched today.

How did this storm come up so suddenly?
In a moment, out of a blue sky,
The day has been suddenly ruined!
Here it comes! . . . It's begun to drizzle.

It'll pour with rain by nightfall,
Thunder caprifies rain;
White clouds coming from the south-east—
Look how it's pouring there in the plain!

Santa Barbara

SANTA BARBARA,
No evil and no disaster,
Preserve us from the lightning,
Keep watch upon the sailors,
The heavens are like sulphur,
The lightning is a swordsman
Zigzagging flame and fury,
Sets fire and sends sparks flying.

Santa Barbara,
As you on high behold us,
We are exceeding frightened,
Afeared, our cheeks all pallid,
The thunder cracks and rumbles,
Re-echoes re-exploding,
The churchbells are all ringing,
All fervently are praying.

Santa Barbara,
Be now a caprificator
Of weather fair, and though yet
It takes a while to clear up,
Keep far from us the tempests,
And be to them a scarecrow,
Once more becalm the weather,
Yourself bring the good tidings.

Santa Barbara,
But for the licking gutters
We wish that all would stop now,
Remember turnips, marrows
Require the rain to water,
Were every ditch a river,
Just keep away the lightning,
And lock it up and bolt it.

Santa Barbara,
No evil and no disaster,
In Malta or wherever,
To us or to our neighbours,
Our mind depicts your image
The woolly clouds transpiercing,
And straightway we point to it:
There, there's Santa Barbara!

R. BRIFFA

The Song of the Sorrowful

O MADONNA of the Sorrows,
Not with roses
Did I seek to adorn your dwelling,
Not with roses scent your altar,
But with thorn-scrub from the wasteland
And with brambles pale and sickly,
O Madonna of the Sorrows,
These alone.

O Madonna of the Sorrows,
Others came
And with gold they built your dwelling
And with stones they shaped your altar—
I alone was the outsider
With no rich man's gold and roses,
I alone.

O Madonna of the Sorrows,
You scorned not,
You the sorrowful in your dwelling,
But you smiled upon your altar
Full of sweetness, full of pity,
You refreshed this heart so weary,
You alone.

The Anthem and the Crowd

AND the crowd stood up as one man and cried, 'I am
    Maltese!
Woe to him who despises me, woe to him who de-
    ceives me!'

And the crowd sang as one man, and made heard on
    the winds
The anthem of our Malta; and the voice was victorious

Over the slumber of the cowardly past, the slumber of
    apathy
When our soul was lying alseep in a foreign bed,

And the ghost of Vassalli arose from the depths of the
    tomb
And cried aloud: 'Now at last I shall find my rest.'

Mirrors ❦

MIRRORS, mirrors, mirrors,
mirrors everywhere,
and from every one of them
yawns a weary face;

and the weeping of the violins
once started, never ceases,
and without knowing why
everyone is dancing;

and the candles are guttering,
the light of many is dead,
and in the heart of the chimney
the hot cinders are snuffed out.

But the dance goes on all the time
and the pallor on their faces,
and nobody stirs a finger
to rekindle the flame.

What has gathered them in such solitude?
All of them are past sixty,
and the heart of each one of them
has begun to pine with time's sadness.

240

But the dance goes on all the time—
how weary they are!
Would you say it's the last dance,
the dance of the dead?

To My Mother

ROCK me, that I may sleep,
rock me sweetly, sweetly,
make me forget every anguish,
make me forget every cruelty.

Rock me gently, gently
with your tremulous voice;
rock me, rock me
thus, just so, slowly.

Hide me from there, outside
the wind is sobbing
like a soul searching, searching
in vain for repose.

Rock me, rock me,
make me forget every anguish;
rock me just as when
I was a babe in the cradle;

and repeat to me the song,
the song of long ago
about the naughty little boy
lost in the wilderness.

'But his mother prayed fervently
to the good God-child,
and He found the road for him
because He is merciful.'

It befell me as the little boy,
I wandered far from home;
and I found everything so gay
until night fell,

and the cold spread all around
and dark grew the wilderness
and lo, I was weary to death,
scared of all about me.

How can you know, darling mother,
how much your son went through
since he set out from home
and went apart from you?

Rock me, rock me,
hug me like long ago
thus, just so . . . yes, thrust
your fingers into my hair;

and sing to me, sing sweetly
the song of truth.

Quo Vadis?

SOLITARY
on the rocky hill
far from the rest of her sisters

in the verdant heart
of the valley
the old carob-tree
bent
with the weight of years
looks around her
to behold
the bustle and the people going by.

. . . And she thinks:
What a hurry they are in!
Where are they going,
for ever restless
from the cradle to the grave,
these prodigal humans?
Where are the roots?
Does the kiss of the wind never tame them,
does the warmth of the sun never slow them down?
Why is a little rest
never for them,
and their sole inspiration
the life of the market?

Ġ. ZAMMIT

The Song of Tomorrow

ALONE there I left her,
Left her there in the black void of a night without
   stars,
In the timorous hush of a wilderness mastered and
   muzzled

By the murderous mastery of merciless whirlwinds.
And I heard her,
Heard that deep sobbing of anguish,
And silent
Silent in my breast grew every murmur of tenderness,
And love shrank away in my heart.

I shrouded her in the shroud of indifference, girdled
    her with the girdle of loathing
And I fled as one flees from justice, as one flees
To cover his crimes.

I left her there in the black void,
In the timorous hush of the wilderness,
In the murderous mastery of the whirlwinds,
And I fled to hide myself in my home
And to find repose to relieve me,
Repose that would let me forget.
I thought in the well-loved things,
The books of enchanting song,
In the legends of love, in the glory
Of the past story of our race,
In the works of painters, or the sweetness
Of music, I should forget that sobbing,
That sobbing of anguish in the wilderness
In the black void of a night without stars.

Like the slow chiming of a bell
Praying in the hush of night a prayer of compassion
For one who lies dying,
Even so that sobbing echoed in my heart,

Echoed even in my ears, like a sigh from the depths
   of a coffin.
Only her I could hear, sobbing, weeping,
Calling, calling: and my home
With the well-loved things,
The books of song,
The past legends of our race,
The sweetness of ravishing music, was a wilderness
Terrified, mastered and muzzled by the mastery of the
   whirlwinds.
And I ran as one mad towards the black void of a
   night without stars,
And I found her, alone and weeping,
Shrouded in the shroud of indifference, girdled with
   the girdle of loathing.

And I threw myself down on my knees. Upon her head
Numbed like the marble of a tomb
I scattered tears of contrition.
I clasped her to my breast, called her by every name
   of love,
And I kissed her.

And the darkness faded,
The whirlwinds abated,
The wilderness was changed into a garden all of
   flowers;
Hushed was the sighing; the shroud
Became a garment whose loveliness outshone the stars
Which silently glide down heaven upon summer
   nights,
And I saw her in her beauty, and loved her.

And she said to me: 'Poet, in my eyes you will find a
    sea of hidden comfort.
Yesterday belongs to yesterday: its greatness
Vanished with the sun over the horizon,
Buried in the sepulchre of its past grandeur.
I am the future. I am the song of tomorrow. My youth
    is your song.
Abandon the gods of the past,
The dance of the sorcerers shrilling in the moonlit
    nights.
There is no song but I, there is no peace in the past.
Your love is for me: give it me—
The wealth yet to come, the magic of your song of my
    beauty.'

Ġ. PISANI

Gigantija

IN the light of the lovely moon
all through the sweet hours of the summer nights
there in the hush of the wilderness green for ever
Gigantija dreams:

Dreams that she sees again
out of the few small huts erected near her
two by two issuing, slowly approaching,
the faces she loves.

They enter; suddenly the temple
is filled with a throng of women, children, men,
wan faces; on each face can be read a look
of fear and sadness.

A voice is heard echoing:
'For to dispel the famine that would destroy us
the gods desire forthwith, that they may forgive us,
a maiden to die for us.'

A fearful clamour goes up,
weeping and sobbing, with the murmur of many
    voices;
The dread of death possesses the hapless multitude
hungry these long months.

But amid all the shouting,
while every voice bewails the grievous tragedy
a maiden, golden-tressed, blue of eye, pale
steps out of the throng

And she cries in a loud voice:
'Since my arms are of no avail against this
I will give to the gods my life and youth, I
will die for Gozo.'

Then the altar smokes
and there commences the fading anthem of death,
the drums softly rumble out the last lament,
the earth is blood-drenched.

The morrow Gozo was verdant,
our fields were overflowing with fatness and corn,
every one ate and drank, many made revel,
every heart rejoiced.

It is of this that, under the moon
all through the sweet hours of the summer nights
there in the hush of the wilderness green for ever
Gigantija dreams.

T. VASSALLO

At the Luxor

THIS time, dear island, within my breast
it was not the flame of peace and joy that burned
as upon a white sheet you showed the audience
with your head uplifted
the hard blows you suffered with fortitude.
What burned was a fire of fury,
of cursing and hatred
towards him who, blinded by envy,
forgot the past history of your sons
and thought that in two days he would destroy you.

The murmur of the people round me stopped sud-
     denly:
no one breathed.
With their eyes nailed to the battle
fierce in the clear sky,
everyone marvelled at your courage;
they heard in unison
the guns barking like watchdogs
when they perceive a stranger approaching;
they saw in your skies
bursting and exploding,

opening like wool the cloudy shell-bursts
and beheld, as they cursed
zigzagging among them here and there, destructive,
terrifying
the wings of the enemy
that without shame
were dropping death from the skies
on grown-ups and children, on the aged and sick too.

My heart was sorrowful when I beheld the ruins,
houses of noblemen, the treasures of the Knights,
homes of the workers, heritage of strength and sweat,
even the houses of the great God, in ruins,
all confounded together—
the sowing of the cruel foeman before he crashed
   on you
pierced by our heroic fighters.
And the people around me sighed and pitied you;
in my ears they murmured
words of compassion.
And I too felt deeply, for before I left you,
my little homeland,
I left you smiling, full of vitality,
swimming beneath the August sun
warm in the blue sea,
and I never dreamed what you would suffer.

But when the people saw, and I with them,
the spattered wings falling from heaven
mastered by the rage of our shells,
whistling, crippled, as they fell
with tongues of fire and smoke issuing out of them,

O how it sounded, echoing and trembling,
vibrating all around the hall,
the cry of relief
from as many mouths as were present!
Then the joyous cries grew more numerous and
  stronger
and the crowd began to cheer and salute you
as, gallant, began to appear
your sons, the watchmen.
They beheld in their arms strength,
they read in their hearts a firm will,
on your foreheads your great history. For the past
is not only scribbled on the leaf of a chronicle,
not only chiselled on white marble
that the proud man erects
from time to time in the squares in the middle of the
  city
to teach his children;
but burnt
with the tears and blood of our dear forefathers
into every child that flowered out of them
and shows in the face when the heart is angered.

And when we beheld those gallant faces
our hearts were encouraged and strengthened,
because we well know
that, left in their hands, Malta ours
was, and will remain forever.
Whereas in the past, little Malta, there were many
who had never heard of you,
today you will not find a single corner in the world
that is not amazed at you

and does not learn a lesson from your great deeds.
Keep on holding back the enemy, as you held back
not once or twice
the enemies of the past. Your hope in God
has ever been; therefore succour
and with it victory
never failed you.

I can hear already, though from afar
hoarse within my ears,
dying away the mutter of the fierce guns,
and in its stead there draws near on the joyous winds
the sweet sound of bells, broadcasting
from all the churches scattered over you
the longed-for peace
over all creatures;
and I see the outraged sky already clearing,
the clouds flying away and vanishing
so that the sun's rays
shall gladden you once more with light and blessing.

A. BUTTIGIEG

The Lamplighter

EVERY evening
as with the twilight
wastes and dies the strength of day,
Majsi comes along with his ladder
and he kindles under my window
a little lantern
which soothes the anguish of the night.

My strength also
I feel a-dying every day,
but darling Poesy
every evening
climbs up the ladder
and in my heart
lights a tiny lantern
which soothes a little the anguish until what is
    left of my life dies.

God defend me, had it not been for Majsi
making his little point of light;
and with Majsi—God defend me—
had it not been for Poesy!

The Temple of Venus

VENUS dwells in a temple, a green temple
built of tree-trunks, of branches and chains
in Sant'Anton, worshipped by all those
                who love beauty.

The dome of that temple is a stretch of clear sky,
its colonnade four laurels trim,
its walls hung with a variegated tapestry
                of sweet peas.

And the water in the fountain, like holy oil
within a hung lamp, feeds the yellow flowers
like a congregation of little flames floating
                on the green leaves.

Poetic Moments

THE sea still and clear was like a mirror;
not upon waves, rather our little skiff
seemed to be gliding over a delightful carpet
                woven of light.

Apollo was at the helm, and the nine Muses
each sat at an oar, and on the prow
I felt entering into me the enchantment
                of the sweet breeze.

God of Poesy! Never shall I forget
the delight of that evening we passed together
in the colourful strait among the fair islands
                of your kingdom.

A Pitcher of Songs

NOW when with sickle in hand
gathering his wealth
June runs all through the fields,
or on the threshing-floor
drenched in light
with a hat of straw on his head
now threshes, now winnows from morning till night,
come, let us go, come, let us go
whither the sun will not reach us;
come, let us go, come, let us go
whither the people will not see us;
come, let us go, Sweetness of mine,

my own Delight,
within the valley of peace and greenness
where already is dwelling Spring
for a long while,
long waiting for April to come.

Come, let us go,
carrying with us
a goodly pitcher
to fill with songs:
to fill with songs of the fountain
delicious and limpid as light,
and of the reeds wave on wave
dancing as one in the breeze,
of the carob-tree and the olive,
of the tall canes and the twigs,
of the songbirds there in hiding,
let us fill it with songs of Spring—

Fill it with songs till it overflows
all bubbles up to the brim;
and let us drink,
and let us drink
and rejoice us two together,
singing the song
of true love
that binds us two together,
within the valley which, we swear, we will not tell to
    anyone,
neither now, nor tomorrow, nor the day after, nor
    ever!

Catharine

CATHARINE, with your great eyes looking so anxious,
Don't be afraid, you'll wed and be happy one day;
And in three years' time you'll have one kiddy walking,
Another in your arms, and a third just on the way.

The Lamp

SAID the sun, 'I'm about to sink and disappear;
Who'll take my place and light creation, who?'
All held their silence; only the lamp spoke up—
'Sun, don't be afraid; I'll shine instead of you!'

The Dog

'YAP-YAP, YAP-YAP!' the little dog barked at the
  moon
Staring upwards with red-hot coals of eyes;
At last all was dark, and the dog went fast asleep,
Happy to think he'd scared the moon from the skies.

The Cock

'EVERY day I wake up the world,' said the cock;
'When I am dead, who'll call the sun in the morn?'
Next day he died, and the sun and the world arose
As if yesterday's cock had simply never been born.

The Fat Woman

POOR, poor Mathilda, what has become of her?
All day she nibbled, all day she sat in the shade
Till she grew as fat as a barrel. When she died
She found Heaven's gate too narrow, I'm afraid.

Three Harpies

THREE sisters, all three spinsters, all three longing
To get married, but it's no use any wise;
Every time a young man passes near them
They cut him up and devour him with their six eyes.

Shakespeare and Dante

SHAKESPEARE and Dante met in a pub one day
In the other world, I don't know where precisely;
Both said how well they'd succeeded with the Muse,
But with women—both had made a fiasco nicely.

K. VASSALLO

Let Us Go

COME, let us go,
come, let us go,
come, let us go, we two together.

Long has May
mid the penny-royal
with sweet voice
been calling us together.

Come, let us go,
come, let us go,
come, let us go, we two together.

You shall make music and I will sing,
we will sing and make music together.
Earth and heaven will rejoice in us,
all creation will rejoice in us!

Carpets of green under our feet,
flowers dancing before our eyes,
song and music echoing in our ears,
one enchantment everywhere!

Come, let us go to a New Kingdom where the people
    will not see us.
Come, let us go to the Land of Bliss, where sorrow
    will not reach us.
Come, let us go to the Land of Life, where death shall
    not rule us.

Come, let us go, we two, to somewhere
where space is not, where time is not,
where in the arms of Music and Song
we shall live and dwell, we two together.

Come, let us go,
come, let us go,
come, let us go, we two together.

To My Wife

PERCHANCE you know not, companion of my life,
that in our bond and union for everlasting
is a new priesthood. Nor do you understand
how compassionate God was and magnanimous
with you and me when He ratified our marriage
and our belief in Him. By this sacred union,
Mary my wife, you and I then became—
by God's will—a temple and an altar

for the increase of children: let the first life
be holiness and purity; the fear
of Him who created them will spring forth of itself
within them and grow as time passes, when love,
even as the root of a tree by itself cleaves
a moist rock and sucks it, overflows in their hearts
and quickly makes them to know Him and live and
      grow
as He wills and our Faith requires.

                      Life
flamed like a lightning-flash in the dawn of time
by the power of the Creator. From that morning
this work of great wonder, this labour of love
passed to the creature: it was, is and abides
man's duty to renew it, enlarge and multiply it
generation after generation. Cursed be he that fails:
it is an affront to God and man!
                    A great fortune
it was for the two of us, my wife Mary,
that from the hands of our first father and mother
this task came down to us. A fortune more wonderful
it was for us when with the greatest joy
we entered this yoke, and persevered steadfastly
to bear it with a bastion's strength. Why should one,
although the load of the treasure be great and heavy,
be afraid and shrink away from it? Why should a rose
of the sweetest fragrance and beauty, guarded by
      thorns,
remain alienated from the softness and affection
of the fingers of a maiden or a youth? Life
has nothing to make one afraid of it: he only

hates life who spurns to carry its cross; or else
knows not and will not lift the eyes of his soul
higher than the stars; he alone hates life
who believes not in the God who gave it to him
and elected him to multiply it. The world
marches not to the better, and finds not peace
because its enemy presses it with this hatred.

When I swore to you, dear wife, and you to me
that we should be one another's in the bond
of Christian marriage, we two became as one tree
in the garden of life: and our work and duty
was one only: that from our tree we should yield
fruit in season as much as we could. We rejoiced
and rejoiced when this tree budded in springtime
and later ripened to bear its first fruit—
part of our blood, of our body and our soul,
very life of our very life. That hour
was for us like to a mystery: you became
a mother and I a father: our love and attraction
one for the other waxed stronger: I felt
no one and nothing would ever be able to part me
from you—you too likewise: and the tree
that had wearied after the first fruit and idled
a short while in winter, grew green again, blossomed
and gave its second fruit. . . . And so for the third,
the fourth, the fifth, the sixth time and onwards
our tree will bring forth in due season its fruit
until time shall wither it. Never lose heart,
companion of my life, when troubles and crosses
and tribulations and the problems of this life
bear down upon you with all their weight: God loads

no one with a cross heavier than he can bear.
Your duty, my wife, is sacred: your part, to increase
and multiply the human race! What worth is our home
without children? What worth is our love, bereft
of the fruit that it should yield? The bed, the cradle
all the glitter we made ready for the coming
of what we dreamed of and greatly desired, tell me,
what good is in them without that? Let us multiply
therefore in number our children—the bond, the lock,
the heart itself of the family. The cradle
is the altar of life; in the family
dwells the union of nations, the holy church
wherein is the duty of father and mother to renew
the first act of God the Creator. Mary,
you who became a new part of myself,
know that our children after our death will renew
our life in theirs, and in that of their children
and their children's children, without end. Even so
we shall not die altogether, nor come to an end;
and we shall bless the hour that tied us for ever
with the loveliest roots of love—of that love
out of which you and I promised to produce
a saint for God and heroes for our homeland.

Lights

BEHOLD, in the evening
I look out of my window on the world
gazing alone—or, better, with my friends,
my thoughts—
at the lights swimming in splendour,
white lights sown like seeds, still, in the city.

What sweetness! What beauty!
Who can expound what my heart feels
at this moment!

These lights sown like seeds in the city
seem like stars in another sky
grazing on the earth!
I picture them as a garden of flowers,
hue of jasmine and orange-blossom!

These lights have something in them of the sea:
a sea of silver
kissing the shore.

Ah, let me drown in that still sea:
and in the lights of beauty and bliss
let me die.

Open to Me!

OPEN to me, mother! I am here knocking. Open.
I shall die of thirst. I shall die of hunger. Open to me.
Open to me, mother!

Open to me, mother! Shelter me from them. Open.
The dogs and the wolves have almost caught me.
    Open to me.
Open to me, mother!

Open to me, mother! They will tear me to pieces.
    Open.
Fiercer than wild beasts the people have become.
Open to me.
Open to me, mother!

Ġ. CHETCUTI

The Doll

FROM off the little cot
She lifted her and kissed her,
Embraced her,
Rocked her so sweetly, so softly.
I saw her smiling at her and talking to her
Telling her the foolish words of the child she was
And longing to make her understand her
And show her how much she loved her, and who she
    was.

I felt my heart leap in my breast
When I saw them, my daughter and the doll, em-
    bracing,
Swaying to the rhythm of a song,
About them other children playing happily.
I pictured that I was seeing my daughter
Not a child absorbed in play
But a full-grown lass
In the charm of young womanhood,
In her eyes
In her cheeks
The glow of happiness and of peace.
And I pictured I was seeing in her arms
Not a lifeless doll
But a baby radiant in health and beauty,
Rocking her so sweetly, so softly,
Pressing her to her heart
And kissing her on her hair
With all the fervent ardour of a mother.

Then again in the cot
She laid the doll,
Rocked her a little
And gathered the tips of her fingers
On her lips, and kissed her,
Then ran off happy as a bird.
What magic reigns,
What mystery is hidden
In the innocent soul of that mother-child,
A little girl who loves her doll
With the same frenzy, the same strength
As a woman experiencing for the first time
The love of a mother.

Why ?

A RAIN of bombs began to descend
    From a cloudless sky.
A great perturbation passed over us:
    Peace suddenly fled,
And we were afraid, and demanded: Why?

Written in heaven, and clearly scored
    On the face of the deep
With the blood that gushed forth from my wounds
    In village and town
I am seeing the one word: Why?

From the bastions and the forts which fought
    And prevailed in time,
Sighing upon the waves of the wind
    Rose a weary voice
That demanded of all the world: Why?

And the answer came like a thunderclap
    With bombs and fire:
The foe is ruthless, and wills to wax
    To the greatest and best;
There is no need for the question: Why?

So he willed. But he paid; for he lost
    And grovelled in the dust.
See you forget not, in time's long flight,
    The wrong that you bore:
O Malta, Malta, never forget!

To My Children

I SEE passing a whirlwind of shame and folly,
a whirlwind destroying the beauty in its path:
the glory we have earned is changed into the madness
    of vanity;
of what avail is blood and tears? Of what avail is trial?

We have vanquished our foe. We had every right to
    rejoice.
Our heart, that wept in the cruellest hour of tribula-
    tion,
gave, as was meet, thanks to Him who gave us the
    victory
and brought healing to our wounds, all bathed in
    blood.

My children, you cannot know what we suffered and
    saw,
our steadfastness in those days so terrible

when, sorely afraid, we heard so many a time
death calling amid the explosions of fire;

And how we waited on every day that dawned
after a long, sleepless night, broken with exhaustion,
for the flash, from a crack in the clouds, of the light
    that conquers
the darkness within the maddened minds of men.

My children, you cannot know. You came to birth
at a time when the heavens were full of fire,
bombs dropping, streets and houses flattened,
and a little away from you destruction everywhere.

Neither do you know how many a long hour
we dragged under the rocks in the cold . . . in bore-
    dom;
we continually thought of you: for with fierce eyes
we beheld Death prowling outside in the street.

I saw your mother creeping close to your cradle,
hugging you and kissing you: in her eyes
there was a trace of sadness and of anguish,
and a tremor running down the nerves of her hand.

I heard her talking to you with the ardour of a pitying
    mother,
innocent children: you did not understand her words,
words of honey, lacking all sophistication;
when you grow up you will seek for it, and not find it.

Those were times indeed when our very life
appeared to be tossing upon the waves of battle,
one moment above, the next under; our youth
seemed as it were buried at the bottom of a valley.

At last, with the strength of united ideals
we conquered Time with the bitterness that it brought
and overcame the proud enemy with the help
of Heart and Mind together—brought his might to
    naught.

Remember when you grow up that you inherited
with your blood a living love, that mighty love
which amidst pain and suffering unremitting
of the greatest events gave you the greatest keepsake.

But if you desire that there should emerge unstained,
warm, pure and unblemished that high glory,
keep as far as you can from this insatiable poison
which is creeping among us. We have masted every
    problem,

We have overcome the might of steel, and triumphed
with a will of iron over our fierce enemies,
but fools that we are, how we have been deceived:
all the beauty of our souls lies buried in a foot of dust.

I see passing a whirlwind of shame and folly;
dropped are the habits we acquired along the years;
my children, eschew all uncleanness and vanity,
keep, I pray you, your honour as Maltese.

DUN F. CAMILLERI

Mdina

How oftentimes from your heights you have beheld
The enemy climbing against you, ancient city,
And hailed how many sons for the last time,
And wept to see your walls drenched with their blood.
But tidings of joy ran; by the well-worn way
You greeted Roger amid the greatest honour.
Again you were captive; in the end, with a smile,
You watched Napoleon's rabble run in rout.

Today, in silence, you remember those histories
And weep for the sons who once contended with you
That they might never behold Malta a slave.
So, like a graveyard, lifeless you remain;
And the people soundlessly tread upon your tombs
Thinking of the doughty heroes of this Island.

To the Mediterranean

Whenever with violent blast you smite the shore
And wave upon wave meets death upon the rocks,
The thunderous fall may be heard, the crash and the
    roar
Of mighty kingdoms engulfed in ruin complete.
Mirror of heaven, you have cradled the events
That built and pulled down the civilizations of man,
Drunk a thousand times with blood in the battle for life
Which destroyed the flower of youth and the wealthiest
    towns.

In your gasping breast you have known the clamorous
    beat
Of the heart of Caesar and Alexander the Great,
You have seen Nelson in battle victorious
Over Napoleon's ships at Aboukir.
To Malta, too, you have brought the hate of the foe:
But you also gave us the very Light of the Truth.

M. MIZZI

Battle Song

August had gathered its wheat and gone in peace.
September started to think about ripening
The wine in the vats, the hot blood that drives out
All thought of repentance from the heart and the
    brain.
The alluvium began to sweep all that lay in its path.
The streets of the cities became like rivers in spate
With death at the end of them. Blood filled up the
    pools
Which the dreamers trampled upon without noticing.

The ancient trees were felled, the rosebuds torn off,
Women and men died in their innocence,
Died on every side, died in their millions.
Whole quarters were ruined, beauty was slain,
Peoples and nations were mown down, crowns struck
    off,
And a great kingdom of terror was set up.

Song I

Do not answer my longing
With the flash of your eyes;
Do not like as I do,
Answer me not with your lips.

Leave me my love in me
Severed from every one;
Leave me my love to sleep,
Never waken it.

Song II

The time will come when my love
Will no more trouble me,
And your eyes, your face, your body
Will disquiet me no more.

It will be all one, whether you love me
Or whether you love me not;
Of present joy and bitterness
Not a wrack will remain.

W. GULIA

Why ?

Why, Lord, the darkness of a sorrowful spirit,
Distress, and groanings, thorns, and tear-drenched
    eyes?
Why blackness in the soul of a child unspotted
And this liquid pallor beneath the cheeks?

Behold, O Lord, the snow in all its whiteness,
The crimson, the blue, the azure of the skies,
The transparent veil that gambols with it,
Rose and carnation—fragrances so sweet!

Is all this beauty void and in vain, O Lord?
The breath of a breeze burning on summer nights,
A drop on the coals of a fire flaming spitefully,
Chains of great yearnings hopelessly languishing?

No, no, my Lord, thrust not Thy servant from Thee.
Give him the peace he longs for, and embrace him.

NOTES

PART ONE

THE following brief description of the general morphology of Maltese has been contributed by Father P. Grech, O.S.A.

In spite of the fact that the Phoenicians and Carthaginians occupied the Maltese Islands for such a long time, and gave their language to them, very few elements of Punic can be traced in the present language which is mainly Arabic. Dessoulavy's Maltese-Arabic word list proves that almost all of the Semitic roots in Maltese have a corresponding Arabic root, while only a few have a corresponding Hebrew one. The grammatical inflexions and verbal forms are Arabic. In the course of the centuries Maltese picked up quite a number of Italian words, especially abstract terms, which are commonly employed today in conversation, and sometimes in writing too. Italian has also had some influence on the syntax of the language as well. However, both the Italian words and some English words (mainly technical) that have crept into the language do not constitute a substantial part of the vocabulary and are easily adaptable to Semitic grammatical forms so as to become unrecognizable, e.g. 'L-ajruplan ta' zijuna (Ital. *zio*+*na*) illandja (Engl. *land*) dal-għodu' = Our uncle's aeroplane landed this morning.

The Maltese alphabet is much simpler than the Arabic, and corresponds to the Hebrew and Phoenician alphabets with some changes. Whether this is due to direct descent or to a subsequent simplification of the Arabic pronunciation is not certain. There are five vowels in Maltese: *a, e, i, o, u* pronounced as in Italian; *j* and *w* are semi-consonants and can be used to lengthen *i* and *u* respectively. The *alif* with *hamza* has dropped out completely, but the long *ā'* is still heard in *a* and *ie*. Some foreign letters have been imported to help pronounce words of foreign origin or corrupted Semitic words. These are *c* (= Engl. *ch*), *p*, *v*, and hard *g* and *z* (*ts*). On the other hand, Maltese *t* stands for Arabic *tā*, *thā*, and *ṭā*; *ḥ* for *ḥa* and *kha* and pronounced as the *h* in 'house' (Maltese *h* = Arabic *hā* is generally not pronounced at all); *d* stands for *dāl*, *dhāl*, *ḍād*, and *ẓā*; *s* for *sīn* and *ṣād*, sometimes for *shīn* which is, however, usually represented by *x*; *ġ* for *jīm*; and *gh* stands for both *'ain* and *ghain* but is not pronounced as a consonant, only serving to lengthen the accompanying vowel, e.g. *ghada* is pronounced *āda*, *jghin* is pronounced *yeyn*, *ghuda* is pronounced *owda*.

The grammatical simplification of the language corresponds to that of other Arabic dialects, especially North African and Syrian. Nunation has been dropped completely, so have case endings. The dual is rarely used, while some duals have taken the function of plurals, e.g. *huma* = they, pl. The distinction between the second person masculine and feminine has been lost, and the prefix of the first person singular imperfect is the *n* of the plural, e.g. *noqtol*, I kill. The preposition *ta'* is more frequently used to denote the genitive than the construct state. There are other minor differences which can be traced back to softening and simplification, but in some instances the differences point to something deeper, e.g. 'this' is *dan* or *din* which corresponds only to the Phoenician *zn* and Aramaic *dn*.

The following interlinear version of the Lord's Prayer illustrates the inflexion of the language.

Missierna*   li   Inti   fis-smewwiet,   jitqaddes
Our Father   who art (lit. Thou) in heaven(s),   hallowed be
     ismek,   tiġi
     Thy name, come

saltnatek,   ikun   li   trid   Int,   kif   fis-sema
Thy kingdom, let be   what willest Thou,   as   in heaven
     hekkda   fl-art.
     so   on earth.

Ħobzna   ta' kull jum aghtina l-lum,   u   aħfrilna
Our bread of every day   give us   today, and forgive us
     dnubietna   kif   aħna
     our sins   as   we

* Missier = O.It. Messer. This is the only non-Semitic word used in the prayer.

naħfru lil min hu ħati għalina, u ddaħħalniex
forgive (to) who (he) (is) guilty against us, and lead us not

fit-tiġrib, iżda eħlisna minn kull deni. Hekk ikun.
into temptation, but deliver us from every evil. So be it.

The materials for this section were drawn in the main from
H. Stumme, *Maltesische Studien* (Leipzig, 1904), and Ġ.
Cassar-Pullicino, *Ħaġa Moħġaġa* (Malta, n.d.).

The story 'Is-Seba' Tronġiet Mewwija' is taken from F.
Magri, *Mogħdija taż-Żmien* and was related to Father Magri
by the mother of President Micallef.

The story 'Bin Sajjied', hitherto unpublished, was kindly
communicated by Mr. Ġ. Cassar-Pullicino.

PART TWO

The End of the Arab Domination in Malta

This account is extracted from the *Storja ta' Malta* of
Ġan-Anton Vassallo, as quoted in P. P. Saydon and Ġ.
Aquilina, *Ward ta' Qari Malti*, ii (1937), pp. 174–6. Ġ.-A.
Vassallo was born on 6 June 1817, and studied at the Univer-
sity of Malta from 1839 to 1842. In 1850 he was appointed
teacher of Italian in the Liceo, and from 1863 until his death
on 28 March 1868 he occupied the Chair of Italian in the
University. Poet as well as historian, he knew Latin,
French, Italian, and a little English as well as Maltese and
Arabic. His *Storja ta' Malta* was published in 1862.

The Alarm

This account is extracted from the *Żmien l-Ispanjoli* of
Ġuże' Galea, as quoted in *Ward*, ii, pp. 215–17. Ġ. Galea,
who was born in 1901, and qualified as a doctor in 1928, is
well known for his novels and short stories. The *Żmien
l-Ispanjoli* is a novel dealing with the period of Spanish
sovereignty.

The Ransoming of the Maltese

This extract, quoted in *Ward*, ii, pp. 219–21, is part of a speech given in Port Said to commemorate the Great Siege of Malta. The author is Father P. Baskal Grech, O.F.M. The historical events described form the theme of the famous poetical drama *Il-Fidwa tal-Bdiewa* of A. Cremona.

The Great Victory

This speech, quoted in *Ward*, ii, pp. 288–92, was delivered in 1927 by Dun Karm, on the first occasion when the Great Siege was commemorated in Maltese. Dun Karm Psaila, whose biography is given at some length on pp. 72–78, was born at Żebbuġ on 18 October 1871. Acknowledged as the greatest poet Malta has so far produced, he first made his name as an Italian poet.

Dun Mikiel Xerri

This account, authentic in every detail, is taken from Ġuże' Muscat-Azzopardi, *Nazju Ellul* (1947), pp. 214–21. Ġ. Muscat-Azzopardi, 'Father of Maltese Literature', was born on 1 September 1853, studied in Mdina Seminary and in 1875 qualified as a lawyer. He wrote many novels and short stories as well as poetry, and by his example encouraged others to write in Maltese. Founder and first President of the *Għaqda tal-Kittieba tal-Malti*, he died on 4 August 1927.

Vassalli and His Work

This essay, first published in the review *Il-Malti*, is reprinted in *Ward*, ii, pp. 192–5. Its author, A. (Ninu) Cremona, was born in Gozo on 27 May 1880. Orphaned early, he went to Tunis when five years old to live with his uncle but returned to Malta in 1887 and there completed his education. He has held numerous teaching and administrative appointments and has written extensively on Maltese grammar, language, and folklore; he has also composed much poetry, including the drama *Il-Fidwa tal-Bdiewa*.

Dun Karm as Poet

This essay is taken from Ġ. Aquilina, *Studji Kritiċi Letterarji* (1950), pp. 100–39. Ġuże' Aquilina, renowned scholar and author, was born in Gozo in 1911; Professor of Maltese

in the Royal University of Malta, he holds the degrees of
LL.D. (Malta) and Ph.D. (London) and has written extensively on all aspects of Maltese language and literature; a
section of his famous novel *Taħt Tliet Saltniet* is given on
pp. 119–38.

The Gift of Wisdom

This homily is reprinted in *Ward*, ii, pp. 133–4, from
G. M. Camilleri's *Omelji*. Bishop Camilleri of Gozo, a noted
preacher, was born in 1843 and died in 1925.

Lapsi

This essay is printed in Sir Temi Zammit, *Ħrejjef, Stejjer
u Kitba Oħra* (ed. A. Cremona), i. (1958), pp. 89–93. Sir
Themistocles Zammit, one of Malta's most eminent sons,
was born in 1864 and qualified in medicine in 1890. In 1903
he was appointed Curator of the Museum which he did so
much to found, and in 1905 Professor of Chemistry; in 1920
he became Rector of the Royal University, and in the same
year received the Oxford degree of D.Litt. (Honoris Causa).
He was knighted in 1933. Eminent as historian, novelist,
and essayist, he died on 2 November 1935.

The Decision

This episode is extracted from Ġ. Aquilina, *Taħt Tliet
Saltniet*, pp. 170–80. This famous novel, described by its
author as a 'historico-social romance', gives a realistic
picture of life in Malta during the last years of the Knights,
the French occupation, and the early days of the British.

The Captain

This story is taken from Ġ. Galea, *Ġrajja tal-Gwerra*
1945), pp. 130–42.

The Bet

This story of Maltese village life is the first episode in
Ġorġ Zammit, *Wenzu u Rozi u Ħrejjef Oħra* (1957). Ġ.
Zammit, lawyer and author, was born in 1908 and holds the
degrees of B.A. (Malta and London), B.D. (Gregorian

University, Rome), and LL.D. (Malta). He has written poetry in Maltese and English.

The Museum Mystery

This episode is taken from Ivo Muscat-Azzopardi, *Triq id-Dejqa Nru. 313*, pp. 90–105. I. Muscat Azzopardi, son of Ġuże' Muscat-Azzopardi, born in 1893 was the first to introduce the detective novel into Maltese literature; he has written many short stories and radio dramas.

A House Upon Sand

This radio-drama was written in 1950 by Charlie Clews, who was born in 1919 and works in Malta Dockyard. His comedies for broadcasting are very popular.

PART THREE

The Grand Master Cottoner

The text of this poem, on which see above, p. xxv, is given on p. iii of Ġ. Aquilina, *Il-Muża Maltija*.

Sonnet

For the text of this poem, originally published in *L'Arlecchio* on 6 December 1838, see *Il-M.M.*, p. iv.

Marsaxlokk

For the text see *Ward*, ii, p. 96. Marsaxlokk is an old fishing-village in the east of Malta. The lighthouse on Dellimara flashes white and red.

St. Paul

For the text see *Il-M.M.*, p. 46. The traditional site for St. Paul's shipwreck is St. Paul's Bay in the west of Malta.

The Old Man and Death

For the text see Temi Zammit, *Hrejjef*, i, p. 56.

Innu Malti

This hymn is the Maltese National Anthem.

St. John's Day

For the text see O. J. Gulia, *Mill-Ġnejna Maltija*, p. 47. The Co-Cathedral of Malta in Valletta is dedicated to St. John the Baptist.

Whiteness

For the text see *M.-Ġ.M.*, p. 57.

Viaticum

For the text see *M.-Ġ.M.*, pp. 21–22.

In the Catacombs

For the text see *M.-Ġ.M.*, p. 83. The catacombs of Malta are situated in Rabat, not far from Mdina.

Visit to Jesus

For the text see *M.-Ġ.M.*, pp. 104–8.

Non Omnis Moriar

For the text see *M.-Ġ.M.*, pp. 121–5.

Christmas

For the text see *Il-M.M.*, pp. 93–97. The author, the Rev. A. Cuschieri, O.C., was born in Valletta in 1876 and entered the Carmelite Order in 1891. From 1901 until his retirement in 1939 he was Professor of History in the Royal University of Malta.

The Maltese Language

For the text see *Il-M.M.*, pp. 91–92.

The Sentinel

For the text see *Il-M.M.*, pp. 100–6.

The Sorceress

For the text see *Il-M.M.*, pp. 115–16.

On a Rainy Day

For the text see *Il-M.M.*, p. 200. Mary Meylaq, born in Gozo in 1905, is a schoolteacher and has published several volumes of poetry.

Santa Barbara

For the text see *Il-M.M.*, p. 199. The poem is based on an old folk-rhyme.

The Song of the Sorrowful

For the text see *Il-M.M.*, pp. 128–9. Ružar Briffa, an eminent doctor, was born at Debono in 1906 and took his M.D. (Malta) in 1932; he also studied at St. Thomas's Hospital.

The Anthem and the Crowd

For the text see *Il-M.M.*, p. 129. This poem was written in 1945 to commemorate a protest made by the crowd when the Maltese National Anthem was not played along with the Jugoslav and the British at a football match between Malta and Hajduks.

Mirrors

For the text see *Il-M.M.*, p. 134.

To My Mother

For the text see *Il-M.M.*, p. 134.

Quo Vadis?

For the text see *Il-M.M.*, p. 135.

The Song of Tomorrow

For the text see *Il-M.M.*, pp. 248–50. The poem is a parable of the author's conversion to writing Maltese poetry.

NOTES

Gigantija

For the text see *Ward*, ii, pp. 148–9. Ġorġ Pisani, born in Gozo in 1909, is a schoolmaster. He has written a number of volumes of poetry and prose as well as radio plays. The poem describes the prehistoric temple in Gozo.

At the Luxor

For the text see *Il-M.M.*, pp. 228–30. Turu Vassallo, born at Sliema in 1911, has been a schoolmaster in England and a B.B.C. broadcaster. This poem was written after seeing the film 'Battle of Malta' at the Luxor Cinema, Twickenham.

The Lamplighter

For the text see *M.-Ġ.M.*, p. 78. A. Buttigieg, lawyer, was born in Gozo in 1912; he took the LL.D. (Malta) in 1940.

The Temple of Venus

The text is given in the author's *Fanali bil-Lejl*, p. 15.

Poetic Moments

The text is given in the author's *Mill-Gallerija ta Żgħożiti*, p. 72.

A Pitcher of Songs

The text is given ibid., p. 80.

Catharine

The texts of this and the following six epigrams were communicated by Professor Aquilina.

Let Us Go

For the text see *M.-Ġ.M.*, p. 23. Karmenu Vassallo, born at Is-Siġġiewi in 1913, is a schoolmaster. He has published a number of volumes of poetry and critical essays.

To My Wife

For the text see *Il-M.M.*, pp. 242–4.

Lights

For the text see the author's *Nirien*, p. 43.

Open to Me

For the text see ibid., p. 84.

The Doll

The text was communicated to me by Professor Aquilina. Ġuże' Chetcuti, civil servant and part-time teacher, was born at Attard in 1914, He has published several novels and volumes of poetry.

Why?

For the text see *M.-Ġ.M.*, pp. 61–62.

To My Children

For the text see *Il-M.M.*, pp. 163–4.

Mdina

For the text see *M.-Ġ.M.*, p. 49. Dun Frans Camilleri was born at Marsa in 1919 and entered the priesthood in 1943. He is an essayist and a poet.

To the Mediterranean

The text was communicated to me by Professor Aquilina.

Battle Song

For the text see *Il-M.M.*, p. 208. Marcell Mizzi, born in Gozo in 1922, is a schoolmaster.

Song I and Song II

For the texts see *Il-M.M.*, p. 208.

Why?

For the text see *Il-M.M.*, p. 198. Wallace Gulia was born at Bormla in 1926 and studied in the Royal University and at London University.